THE
YOUTH
LEADER
IN YOU

Investing In The Next
Generation

The
Youth
Leader
in You

Investing In The Next Generation

Leroy Hutchinson

ISBN: 9781099951978 (paperback)

Operation Youth Reap was established in 2012, with a vision and mission to Reach, Empower and Activate Purpose in young lives. Over the years, the Operation Youth Reap has developed a track record of effective youth outreach in the areas of Evangelism, Leadership & Social Development, Mentorship, Sports, School Tours and other creative mediums such as this book by our founder, Leroy Hutchinson.

Endorsements

Teenagers increasingly face a world absent of consistency, truth, and love. Many of the traditional sources of things such as culture, community, and family are experiencing similar breakdowns and struggles. This presents both challenges and opportunities. It quickly becomes apparent that there is an abundant need for Youth Ministers and Workers.

It appears that when we are faced with such a need, there are two kinds of responders. The first are those who are eager to get involved. Often these individuals are ready to run in and engage the youth and do so quickly. One of the challenges with this group is that too often, they are blinded by their eagerness and do not take steps to develop their leadership abilities. They must slow down long enough to grow personally and professionally to be "in the game" for the long haul.

The second group comprises of those who, for a wide variety of expressed reasons, feel that they cannot be engaged in or are not valuable to youth work. Many times persons in this category overstate their deficiencies and underestimate their potential impact on the lives of youth. Other times, there is the thought that the only productive youth workers are those who are professionally trained or educated. This couldn't be farther from the truth. I often time say that I would rather have an "uneducated" individual who is teachable, humble and willing, than someone who has been educated but is un-teachable and arrogant. Interestingly, a glance at Jesus' Twelve Disciples reveals that these young guys were "ordinary, uneducated men."

I believe a resource such as this book can be an essential tool to help you in your development as a leader. It can also sharpen you to become more effective in impacting the lives of youths that they can bear fruit, not only in their lives but for generations to come.

Pastor Ryan Flemming
The Revolution Church, USA

I had the distinct privilege of being a Youth Leader for over seven years. During this time, I served at the local, parish and national levels in the Church of God of Prophecy, Jamaica. My vast experience has allowed me to see youth ministry from the hands-on to policy level, and one thing is always constant, Youth Leaders need resources. This book by Leroy Hutchinson is timely as it is geared towards filling the youth ministries resource gap, not merely academically, but practically, which is very important. It is my prayer that churches, schools, families and individual will benefit from the wisdom contained herein for years to come.

Bishop Dr. Junior R. Headlam, J.P.
Administrative Assistant to the National Overseer
Pastor & Parish Overseer
Church of God of Prophecy, Jamaica.

"*The Youth Leader in You*"... I fully endorse this book as one that is fitting for this era of young emerging church leaders, especially in the Youth and Young Adult Ministry.

Leadership is always an exciting topic to explore and discuss because we can look at the "born leader" and the "trained leader". Whichever category you fall in, a leadership book should be your best friend to help mould you into becoming better at the game.

Being involved in Youth Ministry in church or any organization is not an easy task because youths are not necessarily the easiest of folks to work with. If you do not understand how to lead them, you are in big trouble but do not fear because this book is here to help you.

Youth Leadership is important in every church organization and should be taken seriously. I have worked in this area of ministry for some time, and if I had a book designed for Youth Leaders, it would have made my work much easier. Well, there is now a book designed to assist you and your youth ministry team in finding, cultivating and putting into action, the best Youth Leader in you.

If you are not yet in a leadership position, this book is for you as well. It is designed to help you get to where you ought to go. It is designed to pull to the forefront the best Youth Leader in you. You have made an excellent choice in getting this book for such a time as this. Go and be the best Youth Leader your church and the wider world have ever seen.

Erraldo Budhan, Cert., B.A
Parish Youth Director
Church of God of Prophecy
St. Catherine East, Jamaica

Youth, Youth, Youth! *Lawd ab merci!* We often say the youths are the future of the church, and though this often sounds like a cliché, this statement is an irrefutable truth. Frankly, a church that lacks youth is either dying or dead! We must be cognizant that in this Post Modern era of relativism, our youths are confronted continuously with various distractions that lead them away from the knowledge of Christ and His service. The onus is, therefore, placed on the Youth Leader to prayerfully inspire, guide and protect the church's future. Over my twenty-two years of being involved and leading youths at my local church and the parish level, there are several lessons I have learned.

Firstly, a Youth Leader must first realize he serves the youth. As such, he should take upon himself the attitude of a servant leader. It is also critical that the Youth Leader learns quickly, the difference between meekness and weakness as the success of the youth ministries and more importantly the development of our youth hinges on correctly understanding and demonstrating the former instead of the latter. Let me explain with the use of scripture: John 13:13-17. In this text, before His crucifixion, Jesus did a distasteful, menial chore which was generally delegated to the lowest slave in 1st Century homes, He washed the feet of His disciples. There may be several lessons to be learned here, but I will only highlight two: servanthood and humility.

The Gospel writers gave clear indications that Jesus was a strong leader and by no means can He be described as weak. However, this act of subjecting Himself to the lowest state of a slave and demonstrating great humility is a requirement for all Youth Leaders. The task to lead youth demands a servanthood persona. It is a conscious understanding that as the leader, you have the responsibility to always put the needs of the youth you serve as your priority! Therefore, it's imperative to consistently pray for godly wisdom to mitigate issues observed among the youth you lead. Additionally, there will also be a great need for humility as the task to lead is not often glamorous, and you may seldom hear 'well done'. The attitude of the Youth Leader must not be seeking men's affirmation, but rather, he[1] should serve out of love for God and people (in this context youth).

Perhaps, Jesus' model of leading may be too great or lofty to aspire to as, after all, He is God! Let us, therefore, examine the life of a mortal who is the epitome of a great leader. Indubitably, one of the greatest leaders we have

---

[1] The use of the word *he* or *him* is not gender specific as a Youth Leader can be either male or female

as an example to emulate, is God's meekest servant, Moses.

The Lord called Moses to lead His people to a land of promise. Evidently, throughout the scripture, the Israelites were obedient when things worked in their favour; however, they were often obscene when things were delayed or did not go according to plan. Moses demonstrated great restraint and grace towards the Israelites, who were often abusive and disobedient. He loved the people he was tasked to lead despite their poor behaviour. This was demonstrated when he declined God's offer to get rid of them so that He could fulfil His purpose through his (Moses) lineage. Instead, he reminded the Lord that the people are His and prayed for mercy (Exodus 32:9-14).

Similarly, a Youth Leader cannot lead effectively without true love for the youth he leads. Like the Israelites, youth will often be obnoxious and insolent. However, their attitude does not negate their need for genuine and consistent love. A Youth Leader has to separate how he feels (hurt, displeased or offended) and focus on what is needed to help the youth recognize their full potential and achieve the same.

My experience and studies have taught me that a Youth Leader must not only be appointed, but more importantly, he must be commissioned and called. I have observed an egregious error which pastors have made in selecting Youth Leaders who (from my observation) were neither called nor commissioned by the Lord, to lead youths. Bishop Gabriel Vidal[2] stated that *"it is better to leave a position vacant than to put the wrong person in that position."* Being able to articulate well or being an ardent disciplined youth does not qualify someone to be a Youth Leader.

The task to lead requires a call and a commission as those whom the Lord calls as Youth Leaders will inevitably face many agonizing decisions and challenges in leading youth. Therefore, the Youth Leader must ensure that before accepting an appointment to lead youths, that God has called and commissioned him, as this will encourage him in difficult times. The Youth Leader must also be conscious of the needs of the youth he leads as each young person has different needs. For instance, many leaders get trapped in focusing on youths' and their sexual struggle only. While this may be common among many youths and should not be ignored, the need of the group may very well be something else, such as a chronic struggle with social media. Therefore, whilst individual needs should be met, the focus should be on

---

[2] Bishop Gabriel Vidal General Presbyter: for South America in the Church of God Prophecy, (Caribbean Conference, 2017)

what is pervasive and may benefit the body or ministry. Kenneth O. Gangel states that *"People can only be led where they want to go, while the leader follows a step ahead"*.[3] Therefore, leading youth ministries won't work unless the needs of the youth are being met.

In closing, I wish to revisit Moses' leadership model. While he was undoubtedly one of the greatest leaders, he made an error that cost him dearly. In Numbers 20: 1-13, we read of an incident where Moses partially obeyed the Lord. He was instructed to gather the assembly and speak to the rock and water would flow to quench the people's thirst. In frustration, Moses struck the rock, and the Lord informed him that because of that action, he would not be allowed to lead the people into the *"promised land"*.

What am I saying? Moses did the right thing by gathering the people as he was instructed, but the wrong thing (out of anger and frustration), by striking the rock. Though water came from the rock as the Lord intended, striking the rock was still wrong. In principle, if a Youth Leader accepts the position for the wrong reason or even serves in the youth department for the wrong reasons, God sees every motive and will not honour hidden

---

[3] Kenneth O. Gangel, Feeding and Leading (Baker Books, 1996), p. 21

agendas or ill will. In other words, *"if we do the right thing, for the wrong reason, it is still wrong!"*

I, Damian Hugh Walker, endorse this book as there is a need for scholarly and experiential literature that speaks to this critical ministry within the body of Christ. I also congratulate Minister Leroy Hutchinson for obeying the Lord's command to lead youths sacrificially and to embark on yet another journey to author a book to inspire, motivate and encourage aspiring Youth Leaders and those who are already leading. This book will certainly be an instrument that aids in the development of emerging and current Youth Leaders, giving them self-worth and a drive to continue. I encourage you, my brother, in the words of Maya Angelou: *"People will forget what you said, people will forget what you did, but people will never forget how you made them feel."* Keep moving!

Damian Walker
Pastor - Church of God of Prophecy, Kingston & St Andrew, Jamaica

The undiluted passion for youth ministry is not one that jumps out at you by coincidence. It is a trait that is deeply embedded within you as a chosen vessel of the most high God; obtained through seeking God diligently and essential training.

For years, many Youth Leaders have struggled to find relevant literature that lends itself to the awakening and maintaining of that passion. Some have even resorted to subduing that passion and have given up on the call to ministry.

Minister Leroy Hutchinson, a dynamic Youth Leader himself who has been propelled by such a passion, shares in this literature the plan of God for you in Youth Ministry and how to execute this plan. This book, in its entirety, will enable its readers with a similar passion for building character traits to last for eternity, bringing glory to the Father and moving Youth Ministry to its fullest potential.

Elisa Craig, Dip.Ed, BEd, Med
HOD NCBI Youth Ministry Principal
Asst. National Youth Director, Jamaica

In Jamaica there is a colloquial saying "If a shark comes from the bottom of the ocean and tells you that it is deep, believe what it tells you." This essentially means that those who have been there and done that have high credibility. Leroy Hutchinson, on youth ministry, qualifies as very fitting of that expression. He has been in the trenches of youth ministry, founded a youth ministry, taught others youth ministry and most importantly lives and models youth ministry. He is eminently qualified to speak on the subject.

This book comes bathed in the voice of one who has excelled in youth ministry. This places this work shoulders above those that write from heady theories. The world needs this authenticity. Dive into this book and replicate a youth ministry that produces lasting impact. Thank you, Leroy, for sharing with the world, a fresh wind of youth ministry. It is what you do.

Rev. Teddy A. Jones
Marriage Officer, Counsellor,
Youth and Community Coach

The future of any living organism is directly linked to its ability to reproduce. The church is no different as its permanence and relevance are mostly dependent upon, along with other areas of ministry, a Youth Ministry program that is geared toward stimulating the growth of its youth membership. An effective and efficient youth ministry is critical to the development of leaders and volunteers who will be equipped to fulfil various roles within the church and by extension the society at large.

A call to Youth Ministry is equal to that of servant leadership; characterized by the passion and dedication of the Youth Leader to minister to the social, emotional and spiritual needs of the youths entrusted to his care. As such, the Youth Leader can provide a platform for identity, influence and impact.

Youths and young adults deserve to be guided by a level of leadership that will see them soaring to their full potential; owning their talents and giftings while influencing their sphere. Throughout the scriptures, we can find examples of ministry to youths, Elijah poured into Elisha, Paul mentored Timothy through encouragement and instruction, and this is a hallmark of a good Youth Leader.

Minister Leroy Hutchinson, who has served at different levels of Youth Leadership for almost two decades, takes the reader on a journey in developing *"The Youth Leader in You"*. This book charts for us a path that will lead to an understanding of the importance of youth development. As a Youth Leader serving the church for over two decades, undoubtedly, this book is not only timely but relevant.

Whether you are a Youth Leader planning to call it quits, a Pastor praying for an increase in the young harvest or just someone who wants to volunteer service to youths in the community, this book is for you. I challenge you, develop the Youth Leader in you.

Tanesha Johnson, BA
Parish Youth Director COGOP
St. Catherine West, Jamaica

I have worked with Leroy in South Africa and witnessed his humility and his passion for seeing young lives changed for the better. Youth equals future, and if we desire to secure our future, we need to secure our youths. Unquestionably, we need more books like this and more people willing to sacrifice for our youth and thus for our future.

Tony Litchfield
General Manager
Methodist Church Manyano Centre
Paarl, Western Cape, South Africa.

There are many books on the subject of Youth Ministry, but not nearly enough. Most are textbook types for college-level courses or to train youth pastors or leaders and are based largely on Social Science research and popular psychology. *"The Youth Leader In You"* while utilizing research, does not depend entirely on it.

Leroy Hutchinson is a Youth Leader extraordinaire, and so he draws upon his vast knowledge and experience of Youth Leadership, not just in his home country of Jamaica but in other countries where he has travelled and ministered. His work is therefore not a formula for youth ministry but a rich tapestry of stories, anecdotes, insights, wisdom and a wide array of experiences gained from working with youths that are skillfully woven together and presented to the reader as a work of art. As with art, you appreciate it for what it is, and you let it instruct and inspire you as you ponder what it offers. I highly recommend it.

Courtney Richards
Global Missionary
Director of Renewed Ministries.

Youth Leadership is an undeniable challenge, albeit a worthwhile one, for those who voluntarily give of their time and resources to this great ministry. In order to discover more about the grace to lead, to find inspiration and strength to continue along this ministerial path, this map and lesson filled testimonial of a book, *"The Youth Leader in You"*, is your answer in waiting.

Explore realistic experiences of one who has been on the journey of Youth Leadership for almost twenty years and still maintains the passion it requires to engage in ministry. This book is the ultimate manual for current Youth Leaders and Youth Leaders in the making who may need practical yet biblical support in pursuit of meaningful and deliberate ministry.

Ann-Monique A. Bailey Hutchinson, LL.B
Assistant Parish Youth Leader
Local Church Youth Leader and Attorney-at-Law

Dedication

To my beautiful family: My wife Ann-Monique and my daughters Renoya and Paris, all the youths and Youth Leaders I have served, those who continue to trust and follow in my leadership, I love you deeply! May you each find your place in God's Kingdom.

Table of Contents

STEP THREE

ATTITUDES YOU NEED

Acknowledgement

To say the *'Youth Leader In You'* is "by Leroy Hutchinson" solely is patently untrue. This book is 18 years in the making, and the pages reflect the lessons taught to me by my many leaders and mentors. It is fair to say that I learned something from them all. It is also fair to say that I have gained much wisdom from just about everyone I have come across in my life, some of whom have been mentioned in this book.

To my Lord and saviour, Jesus Christ, who has redeemed my life and set me on a path of purpose, I say thank you.

I would like to express my gratitude to the many people who saw me through this book; to all those who provided support, talked things over, read, wrote, offered comments, allowed me to quote their remarks and assisted in the editing, proofreading and design.

Last but not least, I beg the forgiveness of all those who have been with me over the years and whose names I have failed to mention.

Foreword

Being a Christian leader, regardless of age, is about two things: loving God with all of our hearts and loving and serving humanity as ourselves. (Luke 10:27) There is nothing more important than continually deepening our relationship with our creator and serving his creation, humanity.

The two greatest questions asked by all of humanity are: *"Why am I here?"* and *"Why do I matter?"* Being persons of spirit, we ask ourselves, *"What is God's purpose for my life?"* and *"What is God's will for my life?"* God's purpose for all is to be in a relationship with Him, and His will is that we bring others into a relationship with their creator! All disciples of Jesus have the same purpose and responsibility: love God and share the gospel of Jesus; our hope for mankind!

"The Youth Leader in You", by Leroy Hutchinson, shares these principles and much more. Leroy has vast experience in sharing the Gospel of Jesus by many different means. Through sports clinics and service projects, the love of God is shown in Leroy's heart by how he engages his community and the world at large!

Leroy has travelled to different countries to share the gospel of hope and lead humanity to Christ. He continues to create inspirational ways to serve the world and bring hope to this life and the next!

This book will inspire, uplift and share with you the principles of being a leader to the young. Leroy's quest to see young people lead in sharing God's word with lost humanity will captivate your mind and develop a desire in you to lead as Jesus did-with love and a heart of generosity towards humanity.

Kirk Rising
International Youth Director
Church of God of Prophecy, USA

Leroy Hutchinson

The debate as to whether a leader is born or made continues, as some persons seem to exude leadership qualities from a tender age. While for others, with just the right assistance and guidance, the leadership qualities can be developed and produce high-quality leadership. Future leaders will be a reflection of our current leaders. The youths are our future leaders. They are the ones who will be leading tomorrow and what we do today will dictate the kind of leaders we have in the future. Youth Leaders are tasked with the responsibility to lead the charge concerning youth development in both the church and social organizations.

As a Youth Pastor and a Youth Leader for many years, I can attest to the fact that passion alone is not enough. Creativity and skills plus commitment do not always equate to successful leadership either. Occasionally, we are conflicted between giving up and continuing; as sometimes, despite our best efforts, our attempt at leading seems futile and results in feelings of ineffectiveness and inadequacy as leaders. It was this feeling of frustration and inadequacy that led me to ask the author herein some years ago, "Where is the book, sir? Where is the guide for Youth Leaders?"

Having interacted with the author in different spheres, two things are obvious: his passion for youths and his leadership skills. Having served in the positions of Youth Leader, Youth Pastor and now National Youth Ministry Director for Jamaica, Leroy has garnered a wealth of knowledge and experience in regards to operating a successful youth ministry and leadership development. His wealth of knowledge and competence is further concretized because he has invested his time and effort into reading and understanding the principles of leadership taught by John Maxwell and other 'leadership' experts. With this background and a solid foundation, Leroy is well equipped and competent to impart to other leaders how to develop the leader within.

This book is designed to help appointed and aspiring leaders to grow as influential leaders. In the pages to follow are years of experiences and competencies, penned to help you evolve and become effective. Youth Leaders have to compete with social media, peer pressure, the music industry and other internal factors; and in some instances have to do so with inadequate training. Sometimes appointment as a Youth Leader is based on academic achievement or commitment to serve. However, the follow-up training in leadership skills and how to operate effectively in the position is often lacking; this book provides the answer to this shortfall.

Now more than ever, effective Youth Leaders are needed to counter the impact of the different social ills in our society. The solutions for many of our problems and practical ideas on how to hone our leadership skills and become better Youth Leaders lie in the subsequent chapters of this book.

"The Youth Leader in You", written with you, the reader in mind, is the help you desire.

Sherika Anderson, BSc, M.A.
Youth Pastor

Introduction

At the age of fifteen, an elder made a comment which I have not forgotten to date. He uttered, *"Leroy, anything that is young will always give trouble."* He continued, *"Look at puppies, piglets and even chicks, why do you think youths will be any different?"* I laughed. It was hilarious based on the context and continuation of the conversation at the time, but that statement was profound. That was the same year I became a Youth Leader in my local church, at the age of fifteen, and I have come to one conclusion; ministry to youths is never an easy task. Despite this reality, I enjoy working with this group, notwithstanding the many challenges over the years. The next eighteen years of my life would prove him to be correct, and as such, I have grown to recognize and appreciate a certain level of validity in the said statement.

After reading a short profile about my journey as a Youth Leader, moments before I ministered at a weekend youth retreat in St Andrew, Jamaica, the Youth Leader asked, "Where is the manual sir? Where is the legacy that will help other Youth Leaders who are struggling?" She had me thinking. That question resonated in my spirit. I started to pray about writing a book on Youth Ministry. I asked myself two important questions. What have I learned? How can I transmit this to other Youth Leaders coming after and even those who are presently working alongside me?

I believe I have answered those and many more questions after the completion of this book.

Questions like, how to develop and nurture your appetite to serve in youth ministry, how to affirm your gift of leading youths, how to speak to youths while keeping them awake at the same time and how to develop your unique leadership styles are all addressed within the pages of this book.

This book is a culmination of thoughts, ideas, stages and experiences. Being a Youth Leader is by far the single most interesting experience I have had in my entire life. Being a Youth Leader is more than a position in a church, youth club or any other organization. It is a way of life. Whether you have been appointed or you are simply volunteering, there is a need within all of us to guide youths. *"There is a Youth Leader in all of us."*

STEP ONE:

YOUR RESPONSE TO YOUTH LEADERSHIP

1

When We Were Young

"A strong foundation of love in your Youth Ministry will never fail; it will ensure an open connection to foster improvement at all times."– Leroy Hutchinson

The question was asked, and the classroom got quiet. It was my turn to answer. I never really put much thought into it, since I was already unclear about this area of my life and I was hopscotching around the topic ever since the seventh grade.

"Leroy Hutchinson, it's your turn!" she shouted. "What do you want to become?" the teacher asked persistently.

Now I know we all have or had big dreams, or what we consider to have been big dreams. I know I did. The truth is, just like girls with their fantasies, Prince Charming and princess stories; boys too, in their growth and development, can be easily influenced by what we see and hear, especially on television. While television programs can be educational, many children spend hours watching different programs, that afterwards, can become terrifying to them or motivation towards unrealistic expectations. On reflection, I think I watched too much television when I was as a child.

I too drew a sense of love, reality, acceptance, purpose and identity from Hollywood and the big screen industry. This impacted primarily how I started with my career choices. In the first form, I dreamt about being a detective. I loved those kinds of movies in which the bad guys usually pay for crimes at the hands of a smooth and smart undercover cop. My only problem with this ambition was that I didn't think I would enjoy being shot at. I hated guns. I hated seeing them in reality, and I did not have any interest in holding or owning a gun.

By the second form, I was back to the options table. I wanted to be a pilot. I loved aviation, but it was more about the lifestyle of the pilots. They travelled the world every day, and I enjoyed that idea. I was having a swell time believing that I was going to be a pilot, but soon enough, my hang-ups kicked in. I loved physics only from a distance, and the thought of how an aeroplane could fall from the sky was so much more intense than my love for being a pilot.

Very soon after that, I was on to my third option. This was a bit more practical. As I grew into a young man, my realities began to change. Still, I hadn't gotten to where I wanted to be as yet so by this time; I had developed a love for architecture. I was aged sixteen and in the fourth form. With all the vacillating and constant change of my choice of vocation, of this one thing I was sure, constant, unchangeable, was my love for investing and developing young people.

I was consumed in my desire to assist in solving the problems in young lives. Like a detective, I pursued this calling. Not with a gun and a badge but with an unrivalled passion, I wanted to travel to various communities, countries, churches and other areas. Not as a pilot but building relationships and constructing developmental outreach missions. Not as a physical but as a mental architect.

I finally figured out what I wanted to do with the rest of my life, for the rest of my life. Right there in that classroom, I found my career. I found my place in the Church. Most of all, I found my place in the great Kingdom of God. Again, I could hear the teacher's question. With this sudden new found path, I looked up and answered her question.

"Umm Miss," I uttered with a sigh of relief, "I want to be a "Youth Pastor!" The silence was deafening. If a pin fell in the room that day, you would have heard it as loudly as glass smashing on the ground. The entire class was utterly amazed, and their faces said it all. Beyond the feeling of thinking that they were staring at me for not choosing a more secular career, there was also a look judgment. Alas, it was out there, and I finally breathed a sigh of relief. I was now ready to invest in that gift. I was now determined to develop the Youth Leader within me.

Telling the teacher was one thing, but breaking that news to my mother would be another story. Of course, my mother was a converted Christian woman at the time with a Christ-centered heart, but her only child wanted to be a Youth Pastor and studying Theology was a kind of shaky news. It wasn't her idea of a career path apparently, as well as other challenges that appeared insurmountable at the time.

The Solace I Found

My Christian journey started two years before that classroom experience in March 2000 at age 14. I accepted Jesus Christ in my life and was baptized immediately, by choice. I worshipped at the Church of God of Prophecy in the community of McCook's Pen, off Old Harbour Road in St Catherine. The funny thing is that my reason for going to church was not one of those miraculous transformational stories that we may have heard or even read about in the Bible.

At first, I was merely tired of staying home alone on a Sunday morning when all my other relatives had gone to church. Secondly, my mother had just recommitted her life to the Lord and was going to church in Kingston. Going with her was another nightmare. Every time I recall the entire experience, it's with laughter or a chuckle. She would give me the eye when the preacher was done and making his altar call.

I was always annoyed because I never wanted to be forced to give myself to anyone or anything. I needed to do this on my own. Of course, nothing is beyond a mother's love, and I eventually grasped the concept, and over the years she and I had fun recalling those days. Still, while I was running away from being in the same sanctuary with her, I got bored at home and wanted to join the group.

Growing up as an only child allowed me to spend most of my time with myself, even when I was around others. I considered myself an introvert until after high school. Throughout that time, an extrovert must have been gradually developing inside of me just waiting for the right time and season. I'm sure that the Church has a whole lot to do with the man I am today. My induction in the Church was very timely and fulfilling.

The Church became a place of solace for me. It was a safe place where I could find comfort and consolation in times of distress and sadness; a place of refuge and serenity. It had become an avenue for possibilities, growth beyond my wildest dream and a new-found family-one that had no biological connection, but the strongest cords joined us.

By now, I had infused myself into this new institution, and entrusted everything to the journey, by the faith, which was continuously preached. Coming from a broken home, it was like escaping a through gauntlet only to find peace. My parents had been separated since I was nine years old, as far as I can remember. Now and again I would have flashbacks and vividly recall them living together.

My mother was one of my quiet heroines. She was a hardworking woman, and I was her one and only "baby" as she would often explain to everyone at every opportunity she got. My dad was too. Now and again, he would tell me that story of how he stood up to his responsibilities when he found out that he was going to be a father. It never got old.

At age fourteen, I can remember him trying to find a steady job. It was a challenging time for them both. My dad and I always had and still do have a great relationship, and I found out that he was very easy to talk to. He has become my friend. My father and I are still close friends. My mother and I had an excellent relationship until my teenage years. Many boys can attest to that part. Although I really couldn't explain what was happening, I remained a respectful son. We may have drifted apart because she had to work most days, even on Sundays and holidays. I was inadvertently thrown into a situation where I spent most of my teenage life around other relatives. I knew she loved me and was doing the best that she could, but still, something was missing, and that's where I believe God, the Church and more so, Youth Ministry rescued me.

My Youth Leader

It was no surprise to me that out of all the characters, roles, responsibilities and officers in the Church; I drew closest to the Youth Leader. She was a young, charismatic, energetic, exciting character, full of passion for God and His young people. Her name was Karen Manning, now Karen Manning Henry. Seeing this level of intensity being demonstrated with such genuineness and authenticity gave me a different perspective on relating to my peers.

Now I must say that I wasn't an 'easy nut to crack' as a teen. I gave her some real trouble. Well, we all did, as young people in the Church. But she handled herself well almost all the time. It was as if she couldn't be broken, and she wasn't pretending. We knew she wasn't faking it. We knew she was a Youth Leader at heart. There were times when I was dead wrong, but she never made me feel condemned. Instead, she gave us time, and we ended up making an apology for what happened, and the love continued. She had become and still is my role model who had mastered the art of being a true Youth Leader.

Aside from the fact that she managed herself in an orderly manner, there was something about her role, responsibility and ministry that grabbed me. It was her concern for the youths and the many issues with which we struggled. Nothing was beyond receiving her attention, absolutely nothing. She would listen to our parental problems and meet with parents where necessary. She would give counsel when needed. She watched us fall in and out of what we thought was love at the time, despite us not taking heed to her word and she'd still be a shoulder to weep on when hearts got broken. She gave of herself, and that's what Youth Leaders do. They give of themselves to empower youths. I wanted to have what she had; I wanted to do what she was doing.

Love, Connection & Willingness to Work

Watching Karen as she worked with the youth group and gave herself to youth ministry made me realize three (3) things about being a Youth Leader.

Love has to be your "Super Power" in order to lead youth.

This brings me back to the story of a great leader by the name of Moses. Moses had a tough job on his hand, leading the children of Israel. He had his moments of failure, anger and missing the mark while leading them, but there is one thing that Moses consistently demonstrated, and that was genuine love.

"You can love people and not lead them, but you cannot lead people without loving them", says John Maxwell.

Throughout his tenure as Israel's leader, they caused anarchy. They caused Moses pain and anguish. They made him strike things and brought out his worst side. He wasn't a great warrior like Joshua, King Saul or David. He wasn't the wisest leader like King Solomon. He was never the most patient, strongest or most prudent of all the bible characters for sure. But if all those were classified as superpowers then I would agree that Moses' superpower was love for those he led.

This fact has been proven multiple times in the scriptures where Moses had to put his own life on the line to save those for whom he was responsible. Exodus Chapter 32 supports this. When the Israelites were caught in the very act of idolatry, Moses had just received the commandments. As he came down from the mountain, he heard a sound. When he approached the camp and saw the people dancing before the golden calf, his anger burned, and he threw the tablets out of his hands, breaking them to pieces at the foot of the mountain, took the calf the people had made and burned it in the fire. That day three thousand people were killed at God's command. It was an awful day for Israel.

Once again, Moses, being the loving leader he was, put himself and his interest on the line for those he led. He was disturbed about the day's happenings, and it resonated in him, that he went back pleading to God on behalf of his people. In desperation, he begged, "They have made themselves gods of gold. But now, please forgive their sin—but if not, then blot me out of the book you have written."

That is one seriously loving leader! Moses' attitude toward God's decision was quite shocking, especially based on the behaviour of the Israelite group he was leading. But can I tell you that this is the attitude we need to love the youths of today's generation? A fearless love.

That is the exact model of love Karen displayed while she served in the position of a Youth Leader. The truth is, she wasn't doing it because she was appointed to do it, but because it had become a part of who she was. Over time, it became her personality. Love is the number one ingredient to being a leader and more so, a Youth Leader. Loving your youths genuinely may not be the only thing you need to survive as a Youth Leader, but it is, for certain, the first and most important, if you ever desire to see any sort of growth in them.

Loving youth is not a strategy because strategies may fail and need to be adjusted occasionally. Loving them is a heart condition. As the Apostle Paul wrote in 1st Corinthians 13 and verse 8 "Love never fails". A strong foundation of love in your Youth Ministry will never fail, but it will ensure an open connection to foster improvement at all times. With that said, I move on to my second observation.

Connecting With Youth Builds Loyalty

By now, I observed that Karen and her youth group had forged an incredible connection, and it could only have gotten better. There was this unbreakable bond at the time. We all would talk about anything with her. And I mean anything. She had won us all over, and we weren't afraid to tell her everything even when she never asked. She got involved in all the areas of our lives-not by force but because we invited her in. Personally, when I thought about it, I remember telling her too much, but I couldn't seem to help myself. She was an excellent listener. Sometimes I wondered if she wasn't exhausted or tired of us, but it never seemed that was the case, or she never gave that impression. We would discuss not only biblical stuff but other areas of life. It is said that people don't care how much you know; instead, they want to know how much you care. It was obvious that she cared about her youth group. We mattered. That made a world of difference to me and the rest.

Karen and I conversed about everything-parental stress, peer pressure, sports, academics and personal issues. Not only did she get involved in my life, but she got involved in the daily lives of all the youths. I know that she wasn't prepared to hear some of the things we (especially me) told her. There was open communication, and we had confidence in it and her. We discussed dreams, visions, mistakes and failures. Sometimes I forgot for a moment that she wasn't a man and 'male' information slipped out a few times.

Those were hilarious moments. I remember observing her facial expressions whenever she was told something by me or someone else to see if it would change and become weird or intolerable, but it never did. Well, not that I can recall. It never mattered how intense the conversation got; she never gave us that look of judgment and condemnation. Make no mistake though, when the conversation was done, we were adequately rebuked if needed, but we walked away feeling loved, accepted, and most of all, feeling like God still wanted us around.

Karen demonstrated that a Youth Leader has to show that he or she can connect with their young people. If that is a weak area, as a Youth Leader or an aspiring one, you must learn the art of doing so. You must connect with your youths, mainly because they hardly connect first. They evaluate, assess, test and try the leader's patience to see if that leader is authentic. To them, a connection is valuable. They will disconnect even before you get an opportunity to get close. They fear being judged; therefore, connection with youths will allow them to feel a sense of freedom to speak and likewise receive advice. It creates an open line of communication on both sides.

When we connect with young people, leading them becomes easier.

Being A Youth Leader Is Hard Work

It was the night before the Youth Ministry's trip. We were all excited, and the final arrangements were being made. Collection of fees and meeting time were a few of the topics being discussed. Karen, my Youth Leader, was giving instructions about where the bus would be doing the pick-ups and what time we should arrive at the church. She stressed the point of punctuality.

"Everybody, please be here early! As early as 6 a.m.!" she shouted.

Without even considering the implications of my actions I immediately responded in the same tone,

"You should tell yourself that!"

Oops! Yup! I said it, and that made my Youth Leader furious. She was distraught. It was a rude comment indeed. We debated for about two minutes. I lost it completely. During the back and forth, it was a disaster in my head. Finally, all she said was,

"Ok Leroy, go home and see you tomorrow."

I can't explain how embarrassing it was for me. All I could remember saying to myself on my way home was,

"Leroy, what just happened? What have you done? You should have just SHUT UP! That was Karen you were speaking to, you know?" And on and on I went.

Again, it was a disaster in my head.

I could hardly sleep that night. I knew I was dead wrong, and the Lord wasn't pleased with me at all. I knew she felt disrespected, and I couldn't stop thinking about my actions or how it could damage the incredible relationship I had with my Youth Director. The following day I managed to drag myself out of bed. I packed and got ready to go on the trip. On my way to the location, I was busy rehearsing my repentance speech to her. I did role-plays and monologues in my head as if I had a big audition coming up.

When I got to the location, I saw her. I quietly stood by until I got the first opportunity to speak with her. Then it began. I apologized and expressed how sorry I was for disrespecting her and making a fool of myself and promised that it wouldn't happen again. When I was through I sighed relief and waited for her response. With that smile on her face, she exclaimed,

"I knew you would come and speak to me!"

That changed everything. Then I had a smile on my face. She accepted my apology in a loving, Christ-like manner and reassured me that nothing had changed and that she was expecting us to have a good day as usual. It was as if nothing happened. We reconciled, and everything returned to normal after that. That incident was a teachable moment for me; a moment I will never forget. I can't remember ever doing anything like that with my Youth Leader again, though we've had heated debates many times thereafter, certainly none of which went that far.

Leadership is hard work. Working with people is hard work. Working with young people can be extremely challenging. It is a hard task. Within our families, communities, churches, schools, youth clubs and other youth groups are countless young people who need our help. There are many, rejected, "hot-headed" youngsters in our midst. Karen was prepared to handle unforeseen mishaps while working with young people. Youth Leaders cannot be afraid of confronting such situations because they will happen.

As a Youth Leader, you must be prepared to manage yourself and your emotions around youths in the times of failures, misbehaviour, tantrums and anything else. Now I'm not saying you should accept the inappropriate behaviour. There is a vast difference. I'm saying manage it. Don't lose it. Put things under control and implement what is needed at the time. You can manage what young people may wield at you as a Youth Leader.

2

Instinct (Lead or Bleed)

"An instinctive Youth Leader has the ability to solve problems from an internal perspective" – Leroy Hutchinson

Effective Leaders Are Moved by Instinct

Seventeen years ago, one man broke all protocol while the world was paralyzed by fear on September 11, 2001. Rick Rescorla heard a loud explosion while working. He looked out from his window on the 44th floor of the South Tower and saw the North Tower in flames. Rescorla was an ex-Army Veteran who was working as a security director at Morgan Stanley and was responsible for the safety of 2,700 employees. When a security message was announced that everyone should stay at their desk, Rescorla ignored the announcement and systematically ordered the employees to evacuate.

After successfully evacuating almost all Morgan Stanley employees, he went above and beyond his duty. He went back into the building to save more people. When one of his colleagues told him that he too had to evacuate the World Trade Center, Rescorla replied, "As soon as I make sure everyone else is out." He was last seen on the 10th floor heading upwards, shortly before the South Tower collapsed at 9:59 am. Rick Rescorla was one of the 2,996 people who lost their lives that day, but he saved almost 2700 hundred lives.

Ordinary people follow instructions, but great leaders move by their instinct. Instinct is the ability to solve a problem from an internal perspective. Leadership has a lot to do with instinct. At some point in time, you will have to make a decision based on your gut feeling. Not every decision is found in a textbook. You won't always have a formula for your choices. Some decisions have to be made from the inside. Rick Rescorla used his instinct on September 11, 2001, and ended up saving over 2,000 lives.

On an ordinary day, he most likely would have been obedient to security messages, but that day was different. Instinct usually shows up in a leader when he or she needs it most. If you were doing an interview for a top leadership position in an organization and they ask how you make decisions, you most likely wouldn't say "Oh, I just go by my instincts you know." I'm very sure you wouldn't get that position. You would have to present management and leadership strategies that were written in a book. No company pays its managers to lead by their gut feeling. They are paid to do what they have been taught for the most part.

The instinct of leadership is the first sign that you have the potential to become a leader because it flows from within. People won't recognize great leaders before great leaders recognize themselves. Leadership begins with self-awareness in making a decision and getting something done. This has everything to do with instinct because the hardest person to lead is one's self.

Instinct Is First Knowledge

At the age of fifteen, I was appointed the Youth Leader of my local church. I can honestly remember asking myself two questions. First, can you do this? And secondly, what if you fail? Now I'm almost sure I am not the only person who has ever asked those questions about Youth Leadership. Some of you might have asked them and may still be asking yourself.

Becoming a Youth Leader was my very first official leadership position, and the only thing I knew how to do at the time was to lead by my instinct. In other words, I didn't have a plan. The weirdest thing is that it never felt that way to me because ever since I knew myself, I always had an instinct to get things done, without being told to do so, and getting others to follow. However, the difference this time was having the title of a leader. Consequently, I made a whole lot of mistakes, trials and errors and bad choices as a Youth Leader in the beginning. Can you imagine me at the age of fifteen trying to get my peers and older youths to follow my leading? Some days were disastrous.

I am convinced that some of the hardest people to lead are those who knew you personally before you received the position of leadership. Jesus himself experienced this in Mark 6 verses 1- 4 when He went to his hometown with His disciples. The scripture says He taught the people, but some asked "Where did this man get these things?", "What's this wisdom that has been given him? What are these remarkable miracles he is performing? Isn't this the carpenter? Isn't this Mary's son and the brother of James, Joseph, Judas and Simon? Aren't his sisters here with us?" And they took offence at him. Jesus said to them, "A prophet is not without honour except in his own town, among his relatives and in his own home." The Bible clearly states that He could not do any miracles there, except lay his hands on a few sick people and heal them.

You will find that one of your biggest challenges as a leader is to lead those who are closest to you. I got a few of those criticisms, but instinct prevailed. My instincts told me to keep moving and be not discouraged. Instinct usually shows up before and after strategies have failed and have to be revised. It is the first knowledge of leadership.

Trust & Develop Your Instinctiveness

4 Qualities Of An Instinctive Leader

Fearlessness

He was only a Baptist minister after all. The turning point in his life was the Montgomery Bus Boycott which he helped to promote. His boycott also became a turning point in the civil rights struggle – attracting national press for the cause. It began in harmless circumstances on December 5, 1955. Rosa Parks, a civil rights activist, refused to give up her seat – she was sitting in a white-only area. This broke the strict segregation of coloured and white people on the Montgomery buses. The bus company refused to back down, and so did he. He helped to organize a strike where people of colour refused to use any of the city buses. The boycott lasted for several months; the issue was then brought to the Supreme Court, which declared that segregation was unconstitutional.

He was an instinctive leader of his time. His passionate, but non-violent protests, helped to raise awareness of racial inequalities in America, leading to significant political change. He was also an eloquent speaker who captured the imagination and hearts of people, both black and white. His name was Martin Luther King Jr.; he was one of America's most influential civil rights activists.

The fearlessness of a Youth Leader is necessary for this time and age. Your youth ministry needs you to stand up for it at all times. The position of a Youth Leader is essential because it brings a precise balance and helps to prevent society from giving up on our children and teens. The church is the only place where our youths gain a sense of equality in society. Jesus confirmed this in Matthew 19, verse 14, when He stood up for the children after they were being pushed aside by even His very followers. His exact words, according to scriptures, were "Let the little children come to me, and do not hinder them, for the kingdom of heaven belongs to such as these." Jesus sent a significant message to us that we should stand up for these younger ones. That day they weren't just there to create a biblical story. They became the story. Jesus' took a radical stance to indicate to us that children are not merely here as a shadow of humanity, but they are equally a part of society. They are relevant now, and we should always look out for them.

The United Nations Children's Fund (UNICEF) is the driving force that helps build a world where the rights of every child are realized. They have the global authority to influence decision-makers, and the variety of partners at the grassroots level to turn the most innovative ideas into reality. According to the UNICEF "Every day, more than 2000 children die from an injury which could have been prevented. This joint World Health Organization (WHO) /UNICEF report is a plea to keep kids safe by promoting evidence-based injury prevention interventions and sustained investment by all sectors. The report presents the current knowledge about the five most important causes of unintentional injury – road traffic injuries, drowning, burns, falls and poisoning.

The high rates of crime and violence experienced in Jamaica significantly impact the lives of children according to the UNICEF. Between January-October 2010, boys and girls aged 10-19 years accounted for 25.4 per cent of all intentional injuries and 27.4 per cent of all stab wound cases. In 2010, 4,500 cases of abuse were reported to the Office of the Children's Registry (OCR), 62 per cent of them being girls. "Neglect" accounted for 56.2 per cent of the reported types of abuse, followed by physical (18.6 per cent) and sexual abuse (18.2 per cent).

The cumulative effect of children's exposure to violence has a devastating impact on learning and behaviour. The data show that children and adolescents account for approximately 26 per cent of perpetrators of major crimes. Eight hundred and fifteen (815) children and adolescents aged 12-19 years were arrested for committing a major crime in 2010, with approximately 89% of them aged 15-19 years. There were 1,796 child and adolescent victims of major crime; 61 per cent were in the 15-19 age group and 39 per cent 0-14. The vulnerability of females in the 15-19 age group is evident in the fact that 1,127 of them were reported as having been a victim of rape or carnal abuse. This equals 63 per cent of all victims aged 0-19 years.

Children and adolescents (0-19 years) accounted for 31 per cent of persons treated for attempted suicide at public hospitals from January to October 2010. The 2010 *Global School Health Survey* reported that 21.1 per cent of females and 23.1 per cent of males aged 13-15 years admitted to attempting suicide. Access to mental health services is limited, and vulnerable adolescents face significant challenges in accessing proper diagnosis, medication or any support services."

Now I'll give you a chance to catch your breath. Thought-provoking I tell you. With this said, you should already be planning on how you are going to get more involved in the lives of our children and youths. It is heartbreaking to know that many adults have turned a blind eye to our children and youths in the society. Youths need leaders who will stand in the gap for them. They need to know that they are wanted. They need to know that they will be defended. Over and over again, I would stand up in the church's business conferences and protect my young people. I have been accused on many occasions of being tolerant of bad behaviour and 'taking side' with young people, but that was okay for me. Youth Leaders, we must understand that although youths have the potential to misbehave, they also need advocates. As young Joshua was encouraged by God Himself, I say the same to you. "Be strong and very courageous" I also say to you, be fearless in your approach to youth ministry. "People who see this throughout the world will realize that even in the 20th century with faith, courage and a just cause David can still beat Goliath"- Haile Selassie. Beat the Goliaths in your youth ministry.

Dissatisfaction

He was born on July 30, 1863, on his family's farm in Wayne County, near Dearborn, Michigan. When he was 13 years old, his father gifted him a pocket watch, which the young boy promptly took apart and reassembled. Friends and neighbours were impressed and requested that he fix their timepieces too. **_Unsatisfied_** with farm work, Ford left home at the age of 16 to take on an apprenticeship as a machinist at a shipbuilding firm in Detroit. In the years that followed, he would learn to operate and service steam engines skillfully and would also study bookkeeping. In 1890, Henry Ford was hired as an engineer for the Detroit Edison Company. By the year 1893, Henry's natural talents earned him a promotion to chief engineer in the company and his dream began.

All the while, Ford developed his plans for a horseless carriage, so in 1892, Ford built his first gasoline-powered buggy, which had a two-cylinder, four-horsepower engine. He then in 1896 constructed his first model car, the Ford Quadricycle. In the same year, he attended a meeting with Edison executives and found himself presenting his automobile plans to Thomas Edison. The lighting genius encouraged Ford to build a second, better model. So By 1898, Ford was awarded his first patent for a carburettor. And in 1899, with money raised from investors following the development of a third model car, Ford left Edison Illuminating Company to pursue his car-making business full-time. After a few trials building cars and companies, Henry Ford established the Ford Motor Company in 1903. Henry Ford was an ardent pacifist and opposed World War I, even funding a peace ship to Europe. Later, in 1936, Ford and his family established the Ford Foundation to provide ongoing grants for research, education and development.

Dissatisfactions in an instinctive leader cannot be hidden. It will spring out sooner than later. We often confuse dissatisfaction with greed, but the two are different. To be dissatisfied is to know that, reasonably you can be more than what you are at present while to be greedy is to realise you don't need anymore. Greedy people can't "do without".

Dissatisfied people can't "without do." Whenever a Youth Leader is not pleased with the current state of the youth ministry, it is his or her responsibility to do something about it. God will sometimes give us a burden to elevate and bring about a change in the youth group from one level to the next, but we need to realize when he is doing so.

Most times, God will make us uncomfortable with being ordinary. Normal can be painfully annoying when you know you were created to do extraordinary things. Our youth in today's society need Youth Leaders who will move beyond the norm due to a hunger for change and a Christ-like dissatisfaction.

Leroy Hutchinson

Risk-Taking

In the summer of 2003, while he had insomnia in the Harvard dormitory room, he got an idea to create a site called FaceMash. He decided to hack Harvard's database, where the students uploaded their profile pictures. He quickly wrote a program that randomly selected two images of two random female students and put them next to each other, asking "Who is hotter?", giving the option for voting. The process was in full swing, and the site was visited by most of the students at Harvard. When the number of visitors exceeded the limit, the server crashed due to overload. He appeared before the committee on computer hacking. Of course, nobody told him 'Well done!' and he received disciplinary actions, but he noticed that such things cause stormy interest in society. His name is Mark Elliot, Facebook Founder and CEO.

According to TIME magazine in 2010, no one else had such a significant impact on the world than the current winner. Zuckerberg's popularity was so high that in 2010 David Fincher shot a movie "The Social Network" in which Jesse Eisenberg brilliantly played the leading role of the Facebook founder. Previously, TIME's 'Persons of the Year' included the United States presidents such as

Bill Clinton and Barack Obama. Mark is the youngest billionaire on the planet who created the Facebook social network that now has 1 billion monthly active users. Thanks to Facebook, people around the world can easily keep in touch with all their friends. Before Mark, society just did not have such opportunities, but now everything has changed.

It is said that there are two kinds of people on the planet: those who wait for things to happen and those who make things happen. If you are in the last group, then you are an instinctive leader. Instinctive leaders don't wait on things to happen. They make things happen. They are never usually reactive but proactive. When things need to get done, they are the first of the group who will jump at it.

I remember some time ago, I was ministering in a community that had high levels of rainfall and was susceptible to flooding. The rain had come, and the river was in spate. During the rain, the electricity also went, and there wasn't a backup generator. I was there in the room wondering what was going to happen mainly because I was a visiting Evangelist in the area. Then I heard a woman from the area call me out of the house. She told me that the roads would be impassable if I didn't leave right away. This reminded me of Peter when he escaped from prison, according to Act 12, when the angel told him, "Quick. Get up." The conclusion is that I packed quickly and hurried down the hill to avoid being trapped in that area. I had a prior engagement the next morning, and it would have been very disappointing if I had missed it. Because of her quick and intuitive thinking, I was out, safe and sound.

Most of the world's greatest leaders are known to be risk-takers. Risk takers are never usually famous until the risk is over, and the results are evident. These people never often receive any applaud at first while planning to take or during the risk. Every Youth Leader must prepare to try something new. When I say that I mean to try new strategies that you might not be sure about, but you do it because you know that it could change the lives of your youths and create depth for your ministry. Your youth ministry needs that kind of leadership sometimes; the kind that goes out on a limb for them. Some of the youths we serve will require us to dive in and rescue them. This was the same risk-taking instinct that pushed young Tremayane Brown, a resident in the Trench Town community in Kingston, on September 11, 2017. Today Brown is dubbed the Trench Town hero, receiving tons of media coverage and YouTube viewers. Tremayane dived fearlessly into a flooded gully with gushing currents to save a 12-year-old child. Without calculating the risk of what he was attempting, he jumped. One eye-witness, while giving his side of the story, reported that Brown came out of Boys Town School and just reacted. *"The youth just come out of the school and just react,"* he passionately explained. Brown further told the news reporter "As soon as I saw him my instinct just told me to help him." He managed to save the child from being washed hopelessly into the nearby sea. In October 2017, Brown received a National Award from the Government of Jamaica for his act of bravery.

You have to be ready when it's that time to dive in and grab your youths. Average leaders wait to see what will happen, but instinctive leaders are never afraid to take risks in order to rescue and develop the youths they serve.

Leaving a Legacy

In the courts, the Wright brothers waged a prolonged, embarrassing and largely unsuccessful battle against other early aviators over who owned the flight principles that made flying possible. Requesting complete ownership in 1906 for their flying machine, the Wrights claimed these principles as their own and charged their competitors with intellectual property theft. Fighting back in court, the Wrights' competitors claimed the theory behind the machines as the common property of humanity and argued that the Wrights' could only claim the mechanics of their aeroplane itself.

In waging this battle, the Wrights proved themselves more than pioneers in aviation. Their legacy, therefore, is one of disputes and obstruction, as well as brilliance and innovation. Orville and Wilbur Wright advanced aeroplane control by leaps and bounds in the first years of the 20th century. Born four years apart, brothers Wilbur and Orville Wright grew up in a small town in Ohio. They shared an intellectual curiosity and an aptitude for science, at a time when the possibility of human flight was beginning to look like a reality. Together, the Wright brothers developed the first successful aeroplane in Kitty Hawk, North Carolina and together they became national heroes. Considered the fathers of modern aviation, they developed innovative technology and inspired imaginations around the world. The Wright brothers made a significant impact in the field of aviation, which is considered a foundation for today's commercial planes.

Instinctive leaders demonstrate fearlessness, dissatisfaction in the face of the ordinary, risk-taking, and they are legacy leavers. We should always strive for the things that will live much longer than we will. Seek to invest in something that will outlive us. We serve in youth ministry not only in the now but also for future benefits. The Youth Leader's efforts will be beneficiary to others long after we are gone. Legacies are not usually enjoyed while we are around but rather when we have left. If you are an instinctive leader, then you are on the right path. Trust your instincts; they may save more young lives than you can imagine.

```
┌─────────────┐
│             │
│      3      │
│             │
└─────────────┘
```

Youths

Follow

"YOU"

"Youth ministry is similar to a product,
and how you execute your Youth
Leadership will give a perception of how
effective your ministry will be."– Leroy
Hutchinson

"Re-branding Yourself"

In the previous chapter, I emphasized instinctive leadership and to us as Youth Leaders who are making and paving the way to transform lives and initiate results. Over the years of serving in the capacity of a Youth Leader, I have come to realize that there are two other vital aspects of Youth Leadership which I will share to begin this chapter. These are perception and influence.

Perception is the ability to see, hear, or become aware of something while influence is simply to lead and make people follow you. Lead people where you want them to go. This might sound a bit awkward to many, but if I have learned anything about leading people, it would be the notion that if no one is following you, then you are not leading at all." An effective leader knows the way, goes the way, and shows the way" says John Maxwell. If no one has bought into the idea that you are taking them somewhere, then you are on your own. You may need to recheck your brand to see whether or not you are being perceived in the right way.

In the business world, a strong *brand* not only differentiates you from competitors, but it also helps to build trust with your customers. According to the experts, a brand represents the sum of people's perception of a company's customer service, reputation, advertising, and logo. When all of these parts of the business are working well, the overall brand tends to be healthy. On the flip side, we all probably know of a company that offers excellent products or services but has a tarnished brand due to poor customer service.

Branding goes way beyond just a logo or a graphic element. When you think about your brand, you want to think about your entire customer experience, everything from your logo, your website, your social media experiences, the way you answer the phone, to the way your customers experience your staff. When you look at this broad definition of branding, it can be a bit overwhelming to think about what is involved in your brand. In short, your brand is the way your customer perceives you.

The questions for every Youth Leader then, should be, what kind of brand am I? Am I a mark of quality, durability and relevance? Only you will be able to give the most accurate answer to such questions. Improving yourself as a brand will no doubt provide the kind of results you seek in youth ministry. This kind of introspection will also help us to recognize that Youth Ministry is a product, and a great product too, so sell it, live it and make it worth your while and impactful to those who follow you.

Make Yourself Heard

During my first mission trip to South Africa in April of 2016, I went to visit my favourite animal. By now everyone knows that is the lion of course. After I was through preaching at the local Church we visited, the Youth Leader took us to a place called The Lion Park. It was simply amazing seeing the cubs and the lionesses too. It made me feel like I wanted to start singing the "Circle of Life" from the Lion King, which is my favourite animated movie of all time. I was at a loss for words. We saw white lions and the usual golden brown ones that we were more familiar with. The funniest part was that I was a little terrified of this park...ok ok, I was extremely terrified. I won't hide it. This is certainly not the park you want to be in, should an animal escape from its cage.

I remember my friend Oshane started provoking the lion to make it roar. He was making the usual roaring sound, and he began to draw some attention. I was begging him, however, not to anger the lions while the Jamaicans were in this park. I still laugh every time I remember that day. He kept this going for about two minutes until it finally happened. The lion responded. It walked slowly to the front of its den and then we, but more expeditiously, I started to back off while shouting to Oshane," You see what you have done!"

The lion gradually stooped. In anticipation, we waited to see what was going to happen. With a very laid back attitude, the beast opened its mouth and there it was. Like thunder on a rainy day, it introduced its signature mark as if it was saying, "Don't let me come out there." It wasn't as loud as we expected, but in my opinion, he never needed to be loud. The sound that came from that mini roar in my view was distinctive. You knew you were in the presence of this remarkable animal. I quietly walked away from that cage because my imagination had gone wild, and I wasn't in the mood for a tragedy, which was just me overthinking of course. We laughed and kept on walking to go and see some other lions.

A fantastic experience it was indeed, which led me to an observation and a couple of questions. What is the first thing that comes to your mind when you see a lion or hear about one? Is it the strength? Is it the fierceness and its boldness? Was it about the regal, majestic bearing? Or is it its magnificent appearance? Whatever it is you know about the lion, you will still have to agree that it is a unique animal. In fact; it is so special that it is referred to as the "King of the Jungle" even though it is mostly found in grasslands. The lion, as an animal, is one that every leader and aspiring leader should strive to learn from. If you ask me which animal I compare myself, I will gladly tell you it is the lion. There are several things one can learn from this animal, but for me, it is its roar that makes itself heard. You will know when a lion has something to say. You will know when a lion is in the house. The lion's roar can be heard from five miles away that's the lion's roar.

A famous author once said, *"You may have a heart of gold, but then so does a hardboiled egg."* You may have good intentions in mind, but if you don't say them out, nobody will know how noble they are. There are plenty of animals that are bigger and stronger and have more stamina than the lion. There are faster animals, there are animals that are even better hunters, but what makes the lion arguably the most fearsome animal to walk the earth is its voice, its voice is its repute.

Many of us never met Albert Einstein, but we all know of him because he had something to say, and he said it. Many of us never met people like Adolf Hitler or Mother Theresa of Calcutta, but we know about them because they had statements to make and they made those statements. You need to know that the statement you make is not just about what you say; the things you do and your character, also help to form your reputation. The lion knows that its roar precedes it everywhere it goes, that is why it is the epitome of boldness. If you develop your reputation properly, your courage will increase as well. Never make the mistake of believing that your friends, siblings, neighbours or co-workers can read your mind. Remember what Jesus Christ himself said in Matthew 7:7: "*Ask and it shall be given you; seek, and ye shall find; knock and it shall be opened unto you*". There is nothing to be gained from keeping things to yourself. Be sure to express yourself. If you know you are not extroverted, you can write. If you know you have a talent or a gift, use it. Go out and make friends, a recluse is of no use to anyone. As the famous maxim goes "unless the tortoise sticks its head out of its shell, it cannot go anywhere."

Similarly, like the lion, every Youth Leader's voice should be heard in every aspect of his or her ministry. The idea is not to make young people fear you but to make them hear you. Do not be afraid to speak that which you believe will edify, guide or empower those you lead. Youth ministry can be intimidating and frustrating if you allow it to get the best of you. One way in which I have used to conquer some of my early fears is to speak what is on my mind and let my voice be heard despite being fearful of what people will say. Now, this is by no means being inconsiderate, abrasive, verbally abusive or rude. Still, it allows a sense of freedom to communicate what's on your heart with confidence to affect change. You will never know if a lion is afraid because its roar is fearless. Speak over your youth ministry. They need someone to speak into their lives when it gets hard. They need someone to tell them that they will make it too. Youths are searching for a voice to follow.

Let Them See You

Psychologist Richard Gregory argued that "perception is a constructive process which relies on top-down processing." In other words, stimulus information from our environment is frequently unclear so to interpret it; we require higher cognitive information either from past experiences or stored knowledge to make interpretations about what we see. Helmholtz called it the 'likelihood principle'. For Gregory, however, "perception is a hypothesis, which is based on prior knowledge. In this way, we are actively constructing our perception of reality based on our environment and stored information."

Visual perception is the ability to see and interpret one's surrounding. The young people we serve in our youth ministry are keeping a keen eye on what we say and how we do it. If there is one thing I have learned about youths, it is that they are not good hypocrites. They will say it as it is. The best way to sell an idea is to first buy into it personally. If we are selling the concept of youth ministry being a place where young people can grow in a wholesome and balanced atmosphere, then our actions need to be balanced as well. Celebrate birthdays with them, visit them in the hospital, and be present at graduations or prize-giving ceremonies, support funerals, and other essential functions in the life of the young people you lead. Know their parents and try to create a sense of accountability. The more they see you getting involved, showing interest and showing up, the easier it is for them to perceive you as genuine.

The Youth Leader, and the roles and responsibilities he or she will carry out, must be clearly seen. I have seen many Youth Leaders in my time not knowing where they fall concerning leading young people, and I have also seen others doing a remarkable job. The truth is, not all leadership requires the same strategy. Youth ministry is a complex ministry and has its down days too. I like to call it the maternal side of any society, even in the

Church. It is where great men and women are birthed, developed and deployed for kingdom work. The whole duty of the Youth Leader is to provide guidance and direction to the youth group and to let them see you doing at the same time. Youth ministry is similar to a product; how you execute your leadership will give a perception of how effective your ministry will be. What people see you do, matters. What your youths see being demonstrated through your life will determine whether they buy into you or not. As the old saying goes, "Seeing is Believing".

Five Benefits Youth Leaders Achieve from Personal Improvement "As a BRAND of Quality"

Recognition

One of the significant components of a brand is its logo. Logos are known as the face of the organization. What it looks like in people's eyes is very important and can either attract or detract. Think of how we instantly recognize brands like Digicel, Grace Kennedy, KFC, Nike, Puma or the golden arches of McDonald's. These logos are simple but powerful in their reach. It also represents the type of organization and sometimes symbolizes what it stands for, which is why many times, companies spend millions of dollars perfecting what people see first, through the form of a logo.

The Youth Leader automatically becomes the face of the Youth Ministry, similar to the logo of a company. Without him or her, youth ministry is a faceless mass without form or definition. The Youth Ministry would only be mechanical and meaningless apart from its leader. A faceless Youth Ministry is a heartless Youth Ministry, for the face is the mirror of the soul and presupposes the existence of that soul. A faceless, soulless company or organization has nothing to offer to people but is an organ of oppression and cruelty, taking but not giving. The face of the true leader earns credibility for the ministry. As its face, the leader feels the pressure of loneliness as he or she represents those whom they lead and that for which they stand.

In Linda Ray's opinion, "As the face of your company, you instil trust in your customers and provide them with insight into the personality of your operations. The practise is common and has been successfully employed by entrepreneurs such as Donald Trump, Ralph Lauren and Martha Stewart. Personal branding sets you apart from your competition and gives your company a unique perspective."

Your youth ministry is recognized by who is in charge. As the "face" of a youth ministry, you become the leading advertiser of any event or happenings. If no one else shows up, the Youth Leader has to show up. You have to work on becoming memorable. Be the first to greet and make visitors feel welcome. Just like the logo can be memorable, simple but powerful enough to give recognition to a brand, so should the Youth Leader leave an impression in the heart of those who show up to be a part of your ministry.

Openness

Some years ago, I met a young barber in Kingston. I was on my way home from work and desperately needed grooming. I recall it like it was yesterday. When I entered the building, I saw him standing at the door waiting for a new client, so I told him I wanted a haircut. On my arrival in the chair, I recognized that everyone in the salon seemed to hate, fear or feel intimidated by him for some reason or the other. This raised my antenna, and I began wondering if it was a good idea to continue or if I should cancel. To be honest, he had an intimidating personality, but I continued nonetheless. We eventually started conversing about several topics. He spoke about his children, his temper and anger issues, his grandmother with whom he grew up, his battle with polygamy and his newfound crush- in his own words "the browning."

I sat there and listened to him the entire time without saying much. My tone, use of common known Jamaican slangs and involvement were all too relaxed for him to realize who I was at the time, and I was in no rush. Likewise, I had no intention to speak in any way that could contradict my Christian belief or witness. I was simply allowing him to feel relaxed while being open with him at the same time.

He finally decided to ask me a few personal questions and more so to get my input on a matter retaliating to a violent altercation with another person and his so-called 'women crisis'. I was anticipating this moment, of course. "So you don't believe I should retaliate?" he asked. "Do you think God would want you to do that? Don't you believe that your grandmother's prayers for you have been working on your behalf?" I said. "How come you speak like a Christian?" he inquired, with a face of curiosity. "I am a Christian," I replied, in a similar tone. "*Really my youth*" he gestured. Then I said, "Yes man," I continued with a smile on my face, "and I'm a Youth Pastor too". Without any regard for anyone else in the salon, he shouted, "*A YOUTH PASTOR,* and talking to me about my women?" "Saying the browning *mash up mi head* and commenting on my womanizing behaviour?" he expressed. I laughed at him. We both started laughing away. Still the funniest introduction I've ever had in my Christian journey and by far the longest haircut in my entire life to date. Almost 2 hours and I enjoyed every minute of it. When he was through with cutting my hair, he followed me from the barbershop to the bus terminus, which was about five minutes from the building to continue our meaningful conversation. He kept on in disbelief because for him; he had never had such reasoning and discussion with a Christian before, not even with his grandmother. We eventually developed a good relationship, and I was called Pastor for the rest of the time we were friends. I doubt he even remembers my first name.

The teachable point to this story is that he never got time to build the usual wall of defence that most young men would build when speaking to a Christian and more so a Youth Pastor. Had I mentioned to him who I was from the initial stages of the conversation, it would have been a completely different story and wouldn't have been relevant in this chapter of a book. He said what shocked him the most was my openness and involvement in the conversation about things and topics that the average

Christian, in his opinion, would not discuss and would deem sinful. Yes, there were times when I had to stop him from saying a particular word, but I allowed myself to be real and to understand what he had to say. Contrary to popular belief, when people know about your background, where you came from and the struggles you've overcome, they can relate to you and by extension, your ministry. Respectfully revealing your experiences in your talks, sermons, or your daily interactions with youths is particularly useful if you have a story that corresponds well with your leadership, mandate and experiences. For example, if you are a cancer survivor, your motivation is an ideal symbol of trust for those who may have similar issues. If you've lost a significant amount of weight, yours is the face to align with your fitness centre or weight loss or health and wellness project. Share how you have overcome and do not be afraid.

"Thicker Skin"

Following the great victory against the Amalekites, tragedy struck. David, the King of Israel, the great leader and mighty warrior along with his fighting men returned to his residence and the private property called Ziklag only to realize that everything had been taken away from them. The city went up in flames, and all their wives and sons were taken captives according to 1 Samuel chapter 30. David and his army wept and prayed until they had no more strength to weep. You would have thought that they would be more understanding and empathetic towards David, their leader, considering that he also lost both wives in this great calamity. The Bible said, "David was greatly distressed." What surprised me was that they turned against David and started blaming him for their loss. They even conspired to stone him because they were in pain as well. What was David's reply in all this? He ignored his accusers and grabbed a *thicker skin*. "But David encouraged himself in the LORD his God," 1 Samuel 30:6 reveals. David understood quite well that in moments like those, as the leader, you cannot afford to lose your cool. He ensured that he shut out all external condemnation and distractions and searched for inner strength. What he needed was self-encouragement and communication with His God.

Everything has to do with leadership, whether success or failure. The buck stops at you. Your youth ministry needs a leader who can absorb pressure because all levels of leadership at some point will require a 'thick skin' to survive. Whenever you put yourself out there in the position of a leader, you should expect to receive differences in opinions, negative comments and reactions to a lot of things concerning your style of leadership.

People will have many views about your personality. You will not be able to satisfy everyone, and not everyone will like you. The sooner you face this reality, the better you sleep at nights. You will need to develop what I call a thicker skin; in other words, the ability to not give a response to everyone or everything you hear. You will hear both positive and negative feedback about different areas of your life, from your attitude, tone, hairstyle to your message.

As the face of your group, you are expected to maintain a professional and Christ-like image though hard at times, and learn how to respond appropriately to criticisms. A sense of humour helps in many situations, especially when the criticisms take place in a public forum.

Maintain your composure and develop a routine for handling negative remarks. Take a deep breath, count to 10 or think about the impact of blowing off the top. Think about the publicity before responding online or in person. When faced with hardship, always remember when the going gets tough, the tough get going.

Trust

Martha Stewart Living Omnimedia was founded in 1997 by Stewart herself. Stewart's company continued to struggle while she remained the chairman. Stewart's audience was ageing, and the company relied too much on its print magazine revenue. Stewart's image took a severe hit in 2004 when she was found guilty of conspiracy, obstruction of justice, and making false statements to a federal investigator after she was indicted for insider trading. Although Stewart launched a high-profile "comeback" campaign after her release from prison, her efforts have not paid off for the company. It has not turned an annual profit since 2007. The company's stock price is down more than 58% over the past five years. Part of the problem was an executive turnover. There were at least five CEOs and five CFOs since the company's start. Many executives argue that Stewart's excessive involvement hampered their ability to make a change. The sixth CEO, Lisa Gersh, announced in December that she was leaving the company after serving in the position for just five months. Despite the company's struggles, Stewart was paid more than $21 million between 2009 and 2011.

People will only follow who they can trust. It is said that people don't buy products but personalities. Simply put, people buy people. Most of the time, we invest in things based on how it was sold to us based on promoters, brands, packaging etc. So it is with youths. They will follow you if they trust you. Trustworthiness is a critical quality that every leader should possess at all levels and especially those working with youths. We have heard of a countless number of situations where trust was breached and we also know the devastation that usually follows a leader with questionable character. A professional appearance builds credibility and trust. Youths are more likely to feel comfortable relating to a person that appears legitimate and real. Emotional reactions are hardwired into our brains, and those reactions are authentic influencers.

Improved Value

We often hear the business term "value for money" but what does this mean? This term is used regarding something well worth the money spent on it. Companies who publicly trade on a stock exchange are valued at many times the actual hard assets of the company. Much of this value is due to the branding of the company. A strong brand usually guarantees a future business. Whether a company is in the position to borrow funds for expansion or rolling out initial public offering (IPO), being perceived as more valuable will make the process advantageous for the owner of such a company. The greater a company's devotion to building its brand value, the better the financial return from its efforts.

People will only value you as much as they see you value yourself. As the value of a brand, personal value is important. The leader must strive to develop his value by understanding, accepting and investing in his gifts. Leading the youth ministry may not always come with financial returns for your efforts, but you can't lose off self-awareness and empowerment.

Twitter, Instagram and other social media platforms of this era have revolutionized the term 'followers'. There are celebrities to date with over two hundred million followers each day waiting for them to upload a new feed, story or happenings about their day or personal life. Of course, many of those followers are not always after positive feeds. My point here is that people will follow other people because they feel like it is worth the journey, positive or negative. In his letter to the Corinthians, the Apostle Paul admonished them by saying, "Followers of me; rather, imitators of me; follow herein my example, as I follow Christ's (1 Corinthians 11:1).

"Come, follow me," Jesus said, "and I will send you out to fish for people." At once they left their nets and followed him. Matthew 4:19-20 NIV. The question here for every Youth Leader to ask him or herself is, "Is my life worth following?" Youths want to know why they should spend their precious time following and listening to you, why they should let you into their lives to impact them or why they should take instructions and guidance from you. The answer to that is in your ability to improve your value as the face of your youth ministry.

STEP TWO:

THE TOOLS YOU NEED

4

Leadership Is Influence

"Influence is your personal tool. No one can use it for you. You wield it and make things work in your favour, so wield it with care. You never know who will be affected by the power of your influence."–
Leroy Hutchinson

Much Is Given

One year on a particular report day, my mother came to collect my report at high school. As you all would know, this is the day you regret all the trouble you gave in school if that was your reality. She went to a particular teacher who knew me very well and the influence I possessed. I remember my mom and I sat before the teacher, and he breathed " Leroy, Leroy, Leroy,"... immediately my mother gave me that look. That look that every Jamaican child fears on Report Day. The look that said, "Wait until we get home," and I thought to myself, this is it, I'm doomed, "Goodbye world!!!... The teacher continued "Mother," he said, "I thank God that your son is not the leader of a gang or any negative group in this school. If that were the situation, then the teaching staff would have had a headache."

"Leroy is a leader," he expressed," and if he wanted the entire student body to follow him, I have no doubt it would've happened." After that, he gave her an update on my academic performance in his class. It was terrific, and I survived that day. Once again, she was a proud mother, but what stood out the most for me that day was Mr Gordon's view on my leadership ability and the analogy he used to describe my effectiveness. That day was indeed an actual *'report day'* for me. Those few words empowered me and helped me to discover further, the influence within and its future role in my leadership journey.

One year later, I became the Head Boy at the Greater Portmore High School in my final year. Guess who met me on the corridor after I was elected? Yes, Mr Gordon himself. He gave me the thumbs up and shouted with a smile "I voted for you Leroy; great speech in there, you will do well." Within a few months, I was Head Boy, president of the Student Council body, president of the Inter-School Christian Fellowship (ISCI) and President of the 4H Club. Mr Gordon knew what he was talking about. I was a leader who influenced people to follow and not just in my school but also outside of the school arena.

Much is Expected

In high school, I had friends who were willing to fight for me if I had only just said the word. I specifically remember one incident where I was standing on the edge of the road at the bus stop with two friends when a bus came swinging around the corner. Because it was one of the bigger buses, the driver had to take the corner very profoundly, and so it came all the way over onto my side. At that moment, my back was turned, and I was on my phone, so I wasn't able to see what was happening. The bus swerved around, hit my shoulder, and the phone fell to the ground. Luckily, it was going extremely slow, so my shoulder wasn't damaged in any way. The driver stopped to pick up a few passengers, and I seriously doubt that he even realized what had happened. One of my friends, however, was so angry at the situation and decided that he would avenge what happened. He retrieved a knife from his pocket and was going toward the bus driver. He turned to me, and I remember him saying *"Pastor*, are you just going to allow him to get away with that. Just say the word, and that's it." I shouted *"No man!* Let it slide, my shoulder and my phone are fine." With a look of surprise, he asked, "Leroy, are you sure?" "Yes", I replied. He then closed the knife and put it back in his pocket, still visibly angry. You can just imagine the awe I was in.

It was at that moment I realized the level of influence I had on this particular young man. What was even more shocking was when he called me *"Pastor'"*, before proposing to hurt someone for my sake. He knew the faith I professed, he respected my Christianity, and he requested prayer and my counsel on numerous occasions. Still, he sought to avenge my situation through an avenue he thought was justified enough, however wrong. I couldn't allow him to do such a thing, no matter how I felt. I was responsible for the impact and influence I had on his life. Much was at stake here. Much was expected of me at that given moment.

The Gospels in the New Testament recorded a similar situation with Jesus and His disciples, more so Peter. More directly, Jesus' experience was more violent and graphic than mine. Jesus was about to be arrested, and Peter decided to handle things his way/ out of respect for his Master. Jesus knew the level of influence he had on all his disciples and especially on Peter. The events in the Garden of Gethsemane and the commands of Jesus there taught the disciples nonaggression despite Peter's determination to demonstrate his love and respect for Christ, his saviour.

With Great Power Comes Great Responsibility

"With Great Power Comes Great Responsibility" is a quote said by Benjamin Parker, a character more commonly known as "Uncle Ben" in the Marvel comic series "Spider-Man". The origin of this quote dates back centuries, and the earliest use of the phrase on the Internet is unknown. One of its first notable appearances

in contemporary pop culture can be attributed to a heartfelt scene from the 2002 *Spider-Man* superhero film where Uncle Ben says the line to Peter Parker, Spiderman, shortly before getting killed by a carjacker.

The quote is often mentioned in a direct reference to the superhero's love affair with his only crush, Mary Jane Watson. Parker finally realized that he would continuously be in demand to engage villains and attract unknown enemies. Consequently, the woman he loved would be at risk and a target for all his enemies. This forced Parker to be more responsible with his superhero abilities as it relates to those he affected and influenced.

Jesus addressed those who have been empowered to lead others. He reminded us in Luke Chapter 12:48 when he said; "To whom much is given, much is expected." You have been given the opportunity to influence others.

Get In The Ring, Get The Job Done

In the movie *"Gladiate"*, Maximus played by (Russell Crowe) is one of the Roman army's most capable and trusted generals and a principal advisor to the emperor, but he is set to be executed. He escapes but is captured by slave traders. Renamed Spaniard and forced to become a gladiator, Maximus needed to battle until death with other men for the amusement of paying audiences. His battle skills serve him well, and he becomes one of the most famous and admired men for fighting in the Colosseum.

Determined to avenge himself against the man who took away his freedom and laid waste to his family, Maximus believes that he can use his influence and skill in the ring to avenge the loss of his family and former glory. As the gladiator begins to challenge his rule, Commodus the empire's devious son, played by (Joaquin Phoenix) who ascends to the throne, decides to put his fighting mettle to the test by squaring off with Maximus in a battle to the death. In the end, Maximus prevailed, and justice was served. His influence, leadership and fighting skills earned him a resounding victory in the ring.

Like Maximus the Gladiator, some of us have been in a similar position. Many Youth Leaders were plunged into youth ministry at the initial stage of appointment without reasonable consideration. They were given a mammoth task with very little skill, support or experience. They had to pull on their natural strength, passion for God and the youth group, influence and any other available assistance. Influence is your personal tool. No one can use it for you. You wield it and make things work in your favour, so wield it with care. You never know who will be affected by the power of your influence. With your influence, you can either build up or destroy your youth ministry so choose carefully.

Influencers Cannot Be Hidden

You can always tell who will emerge as the leader from a given group through careful observation. If you give close attention, you will see the one who commands followers through influence. Most of us were thrown into what felt like a ring of young people like the Roman gladiator, and we were expected to win. The hilarious thought was, you were unarmed, and you were not supposed to get out until the mission was accomplished. There were no rules of engagement; neither were there any referees. You just had to make the calls as you went along.

This reminds me of the day I met a group of young men on a football field and felt a need to pray with them. I was patiently waiting for the game to end but watching and being entertained at the same time. I knew none of the guys on the field, and they had no prior knowledge of who I was either, so I was preparing my approach mentally. I also knew that if I were going to get through to them, I would have to find one of their peers, someone on the field to help me accomplish my task in communicating with these guys. In other words, I needed to find out who they all saw as the leader. I needed to foresee someone whom they perceived to be their leader and influencer there and then.

I stood there for about three minutes until I recognized something significant about one of the young men on the field. Interestingly, they didn't have a referee, so there was no official decision-maker in the game. This youngster was the one making the calls, and he was also playing. I noticed that whenever a decision was to be made, he would stop the game and awarded him or the opposing team the ball in the event of a foul, corner, handball etc. Without a doubt, he was the established leader on that field. Finally, I had found the leader. I quietly went to the sideline and called him over. I gave him a pleasant look and told him I was impressed that the game was being run in such an orderly manner. I told him I admired his influence on the group and that I am a youth pastor and would like to pray for the guys. His immediate reply was, "Pastor, that's not a problem; when do you want that to happen?" I said, "I wouldn't mind right now because I won't take long." He then told me to hold on for a few minutes, summoned the guys for prayer and introduced me to the group. Of course, there were a few who were wondering what was happening and tried to be disruptive at the beginning, but he handled the matter, and everyone was now tuned in. I prayed and spoke with them promptly as I had promised, and they were very grateful at the end of the session, especially the influencer. I went on my way, and they carried on with their game.

How To Identify Influencers

A Youth Leader has to learn how to spot hidden influencers from a distance. If you focus long enough on your youth group, you will be able to identify potential leaders, because Influence is the single most important attribute in any leader. In the most straightforward words, influence is the ability to make people do what you want them to do, whether good or bad. Based on my observation with the group of guys I mentioned in the previous paragraph, here are three ways to identify influencers.

Attention

First of all, an influencer gets people's attention if not all the time, most of the time. This is because they are usually not afraid to show themselves and their ability to affect change in a given area or situation. They are often the ones who stand up and stand out despite the crowd.

For the most part, those who get the attention of the crowd are the ones who have the highest chances of impacting the crowd. We can only affect people if they see us. Seeing is believing for many. There are many young influencers right under our noses, in our churches, workplaces, and communities, and they are waiting to be discovered. If and when they get your attention, do not ignore them. Instruct them on how to see the bigger picture of leadership, demonstrate for them the art of becoming a leader and most of all help them to grab other's attention because that is how they will continuously be discovered.

Answers

The second trait of an influencer should be very familiar to many of us. You can conclude that a person is an influencer by observing that others look to them for answers. It is not that they always have the answers but people always think that they do. This forces them to become solution-oriented, creative individuals and strong advisors in times of adversities. How many of us have that one member in your family, group or church, who is always being asked, *"So what are we going to do about this?"*

I have seen such recurrences several times and also had experiences personally, and I'm pretty sure you have too. When the going gets tough, the tough get the questions. Look out for the one who gets the questions and you will be able to identify a potential influencer.

Entourage

Thirdly, whether they are introverted or extroverted, influencers always get people to rally behind them. They have an entourage with them. They might not be the talker either, but they sure are usually the decision-makers in the group. The youths of today's society want to follow someone. They crave leadership and they are searching for someone to lead them. Sad to say, many of our youth are being led down the wrong path. With an uncontrollable amount of mixed leadership in our society, it's tough for some young people to decide which entourage they should join. This is where we see the influencers surfacing and pulling to themselves followers. Look in your surrounding and identify those who possess the qualities of an influencer, especially those who command people to join them in whatever they set out to do.

If you question your own leadership and want to find out if you still can lead people, check your influence. Rethink and if you still can get people's attention, create answers and form an entourage. If those are your findings, then yes, if you are still making any form of impact, you can still lead. As long as people are still willing to be influenced by you, then you can still be a leader.

Vision Is Your Springboard

"Your youth ministry will not survive without vision; neither can it grow beyond your vision for it. As the leader, you are the visionary of the organization. What you see is important. What you see will determine where and how far you go." – Leroy Hutchinson

I t all began with a vision. In June of 1956, Loren Cunningham, a 20-year-old student from the United States, spent a part of his summer break in Nassau, Bahamas touring with a singing group. One night after a busy day, Loren had an unusual experience. "I lay down on the bed," he recalled, "doubled the pillow under my head and opened my Bible, routinely asking God to speak into my mind. What happened next was far from routine.

Suddenly, I was looking up at a map of the world. Only the map was alive, moving! I sat up. I shook my head, rubbed my eyes. It was a mental movie. I could see all the continents. Waves were crashing onto the shores. Each went onto a continent, then receded, then came up further until it covered the continent completely. I caught my breath. Then, as I watched, the scene changed. The waves became young people–kids my age and even younger–covering the continents. They were talking to people on the street corners and outside bars.

They were going house to house. They were preaching. 'Was that really you, Lord?' I wondered, still staring at the wall, amazed. Young people–kids really–going out as missionaries! What an idea! And I thought 'Why did God give me this vision?"

In the summer of 1960, Loren graduated from college. With the vision still on his mind, Loren led a youth mission trip to Hawaii. While there, he developed more of the vision for a new organization. This ministry would send young people out after high school to gain a sense of purpose.

It would welcome all Christians no matter what their denomination. He started that organization, Youth With A Mission, by the end of the year. Two years later, Loren married Darlene Scratch. By 1966, YWAM had grown to 10 full-time staff and now attracted hundreds of summer short-term volunteers. YWAM teams were being sent to the West Indies, Samoa, Hawaii, Mexico, and Central America. Together, Loren and Darlene are viewed as co-founders of YWAM today.

What You Can See Is What You Get

A clear vision is an important aspect of the Youth Leader's life and his or her ministry. Whatsoever you set out to accomplish must be embedded in vision, mission and proper planning. Your vision will propel you into greatness. It might not be enough to take you everywhere, but without vision, you certainly can't go anywhere. We usually see before we apprehend. Your vision is similar to a springboard. You jump on it and it takes higher. It allows you to see from an unusual altitude and affords you the opportunity to not only dream but dream big. It takes you to places you would have never gone before and inspires you to become a better you.

Loren kept the vision that he had received for four years before making it into a reality, but the most important thing was that he had a vision. The Bible reveals to us the danger of a people living without a vision and how it can destroy such lives. Proverbs 29:18 says, "Where there is no vision, the people perish." Your youth ministry will not survive without vision; neither can it grow beyond your vision for it. As the leader, you are the visionary of the organization. What you see is important. What you see will determine where and how far you go.

Where there is no vision, we have no chance of a higher altitude. Vision is to see something in its impossible state before it becomes possible. My objective for this chapter is to have my readers discover and come to a place of realization that being a successful Youth Leader walks hand in hand with the size of your vision for yourself and those you serve and lead.

Sight vs Vision

At the age of nine, Marla Runyan developed Stargardts, a disease that left her legally blind but still having her peripheral vision. While studying at San Diego State University, she began competing in several athletic disciplines; the heptathlon, high jump and shot put, to name a few.

In 1999 at the Pan American Games, Runyan cemented herself as a world-class runner by winning the 1500 metre race. Just a year later, she became the first legally blind athlete to compete in the Olympics, achieving the highest finish by an American woman in the 1,500-metre event. In the following year, Marla was crowned the USA 5K outdoor champion, a feat which she repeated the next year.

Marla is possibly one of the most versatile and well-rounded athletes ever to compete and win at national and world-class levels. She held records in the 20km, 500m, Female Marathon and Heptathlon. Not only is she an exceptional Olympian, but Marla is also dedicated to supporting other blind people, and has been an ambassador for the Perkins School for the Blind since 2001. She also released her autobiography "No Finish Line: My Life As I See It". In 2002, she added the road 5K and 10K National Championships and married her coach, Matt Lonergan.

Similarly, this singer was blind from infancy. At age twelve he signed with Motown Records as a pre-adolescent and continues to perform and record for the label. It is thought that he received excessive oxygen in his incubator which led to retinopathy of prematurity, a destructive ocular disorder affecting the retina, characterized by abnormal growth of blood vessels, scarring, and sometimes retinal detachment. All those diagnoses and realities never stopped him from fulfilling his dreams. He is the American singer-songwriter, multi-instrumentalist, and record producer Stevie Wonder.

"The only thing worse than being blind is having sight but no vision," says Helen Keller. As you can see from these remarkable visionaries, turning blind, or being born without sight, does not mean a lesser life. These are only two of the many inspirational stories of visually impaired world changers. Whether this involves scaling the world's tallest peaks or pioneering charities to enrich and empower other visually impaired people, these two inspirational people have done it all.

Marla Runyan perfectly encapsulates their spirit, drive and ambition; blindness is a matter of perception. Both

Marla and Stevie were faced with blindness at an early stage of life. They could have given up on life. They both had reasons as far as many would think, to throw their hands up and yield to the thought of not being significant people in the world, but they didn't. Their loss of sight wasn't enough to keep them from having a set vision for their lives. They still had what many people with visual capability do not have, a determination to live their dreams despite their inability to see the outside world. They had an inner world that was motivating them to go beyond their visually impaired reality. They still had a vision within.

Think It, See it, Do it

Some time ago, I was having a discussion with my mentor, Rev. Courtney Richards, who exclaimed, "Son, your vision is only as large or small as the size of your mind." My eyes popped open. That was food for thought. He continued by saying, "If you're not willing to think it, you're not going to be able to envision it, and certainly you're not going to able to do it. How much are you willing to expand your thinking?" I grabbed my pen with a smile on my face. He then laughed and said, "I know you, Leroy, you're going to run with that one,

115

aren't you?" Of course, I did. Within seconds I wrote it down while still talking to him. "I already did, "I told him, and we both had a good laugh and continued with the conversation.

The Thinker

Thinkers are emotionally intelligent people. Your youth ministry needs a thinker, and you have to be that person. A leader, who thinks about developing their ministry, will undoubtedly arrive at solutions more rapidly than one who doesn't. Thinkers are people who never underestimate the power of their mind. The mind is a terrible thing to waste, I have often heard. Everything starts from the mind, including major corporations.

According to Harvey Deutschendorf, an emotional intelligence expert, author and speaker "Many people believe that creativity and innovative thinking are traits that we are born with—we either have them or not. However, we have found that highly innovative people are a work in progress, forever questioning and examining themselves and the world around them. Far from being something we are born with, we can all become more innovative and creative by developing the traits that innovative people share."

Here are some of the emotional intelligence-related attributes that innovative people share, according to Harvey.

1. Innovative Thinkers Have Their Ego In Check

Emotionally intelligent people have their egos under control and are open to other people's ideas. They don't think their ideas are always the best. As a result of their openness to other ideas, they can accumulate a more extensive source of data from which to draw. They are also less likely to fall into the trap of following up on ideas and prospects that are only popular and then receiving kudos for them.

2. Confident And Not Arrogant

Even though they may not think their ideas are always spot on, there is always a belief in their craft, and they innovate accordingly. They see failures as temporary setbacks. By failing, this will uncover a way that doesn't work, bringing them closer to a way that will. Great innovators such as Edison, failed countless times before achieving a breakthrough that led to success. A common factor in all innovators is that they see failures and setbacks as temporary and do not take them personally.

3. They Are Continually Curious

Emotionally intelligent people are curious about people, concepts, and issues. They're open to new information always on the lookout for new ideas that can be put into practice. Being avid readers, forever seeking out new ideas, and expanding their knowledge base increases their repertoire of tools for future use. Noticing every opportunity-a random meeting with a stranger, a conversation, or an event they are attending are always occasions to learn something new. Every person they talk to is seen as possessing some knowledge that may be beneficial to them.

4. They Are Good Listeners

Emotionally intelligent people pick up on information and can sit back and take it in, and are adept at processing information that makes them excellent listeners. When someone is speaking, most people are formulating a response in their minds instead of just focusing upon what the person talking is saying. Good listeners can focus not only on the words that are being spoken but are aware of the tone of the words, the body language expressed, and the emotions behind them. This allows the individual to not only absorb valuable information but develop strong relationships with others. We all have a strong desire to be heard and are attracted to those we feel have taken the time and effort to listen to us.

5. They Guard Their Emotions Against Their Decisions

Emotionally intelligent people see failure as a process — this takes them one step closer to being their best self. They don't have to defend an idea that is proven to be wrong as they're seeking to advance themselves personally and are looking to improve their ideas. Emotionally intelligent people just love to create because this fills their soul and life with purpose.

6. They Take Directions

Emotionally intelligent people have a keen sense of awareness. They can express their emotions in a way that isn't confrontational. They can be assertive without being aggressive. One must be able to take direction in order to give direction.

7. They Empathize

Being emotionally intelligent allows people to feel comfortable around you. To truly understand a customer's needs, you have to have empathy. It's not just about the product. It's about the people. As Maya Angelou said, "You may not remember what someone said to you, but you will remember how they made you feel."

The Visionary

Your vision can leave you in lonely places. Men of vision are often lonely people until others buy into their vision and make common cause with them. There is a significant difference between the thought and turning it into a vision. Nehemiah must have been lonely that night when he walked around the ruined walls and burnt out gates of Jerusalem with a vision for the rebuilding of the city. He was lonely, that is until he shared his vision with the leaders of the city and drew them into it. How glad he was when they replied echoing his challenge, "Let us arise and build!"

Being the leader and the visionary that you are carries with it a certain 'weight'. It is important that as leaders, we see the downside of leadership, especially where loneliness is concerned. I have had my lonely days too and still do from time to time. Sometimes solitude is necessary for the vision to be birthed or managed. Alfred Horsford puts it this way, in his precious piece *LONELINESS IN LEADERSHIP:*

"Leadership is by its very nature a lonely business. It is self-evident that loneliness goes with the territory. It is one of the occupational hazards of leadership. Leaders alone bear the blame or burden or are expected to find solutions when crises arise in the group. As indicated by Truman, the leader cannot shift the blame to others. The buck stops right here, on his desk. In the words of the old negro spiritual:

He has to walk that lonesome valley,

He has to walk it by himself;

O nobody else can walk it for him,

He has to walk it by himself.

With respect to the Church, the leader is the one who hears from God.

Consequently, like a Moses, an Isaiah, a Jeremiah, or a Saul he stands alone in God's 'presence on behalf of his people. They come to him and ask, "Is there a word from the Lord?" He must be able to answer, "Thus saith the Lord." "when there is no word from God, he alone feels the burden of a quiet sense of desperation. He alone waits in prayer and fasting until the answer comes.

121

Many in sacred and secular history have felt the loneliness of leadership: Elijah under his juniper tree fleeing from Jezebel after a great victory. Moses in the face of a murmuring, mutinous multitude. David in the lion's den in Babylon. Job in his ash-heap after losing possessions, family, and friends. Jesus on the cross, forsaken by God and men. Abraham leading his son to be an offering to God on Mt. Moriah. Jacob standing at Jabbok dreading the meeting with his brother Esau. Washington in Valley Forge before confronting the British. General Eisenhower before the Normandy Invasion.Alfred the Great after being defeated by the Danes.Sir Paul Scoon as Governor-General in the face of a military push.

Loneliness is not without its positive results. Great plans are forged in the fiery furnace of loneliness. Out of the travail of loneliness is born new vision, high ideals, brilliant strategies, and noble endeavours. It was while alone in Valley Forge in prayer that Washington gained wisdom and gathered the courage to regroup and attack the British. That period of loneliness ultimately led to success in the Revolutionary War. Robert the Bruce, watching a spider alone in a cave in Scotland gathered the courage and inspiration to win the victory against the English at Bannockburn.

From the loneliness of a laboratory, lake-side or library have come experiments and ideas that have rocked the world, defined technology, won battles and changed the face of society. The canny leader can use loneliness creatively and constructively.

Dietrich Bonhoeffer must have been lonely as he languished in prison awaiting execution by the Nazi for complicity in an attempt to take out Hitler. It was lonely to walk a path of discipleship that was unique, but he continues to inspire many to embrace their own path and demonstrate faithfulness to Jesus Christ.

Richard Wurmbrant felt the sting of loneliness while being tortured in a prison in Romania for daring to take a principled stand against Communism.

In the movie, A Woman Called Moses, in which Cecily Tyson acted as Harriet Tubman it was lonely business when this courageous woman risked her life to save hundreds as she came stealthily by night to lead them to safety. They awaited the sound of her voice as she would sing, 'Swing low sweet chariot, coming for to carry me home."

It was lonely when Rosa Parks resisted an apartheid culture and chose to retain her seat on the bus instead of surrendering it to a white person.

Winston Churchill showed rare courage in loneliness when called to lead Britain against Nazi Germany. As he faced his fearful and anxious cabinet, he cried, "Gentlemen, I find this exhilarating."

Mother Teresa knew loneliness as she went through the "dark night of the soul" even while she was ministering to others in India those many years.

It was lonely for Nelson Mandela when he lay languishing in prison on Robin Island for resisting the apartheid South African government. His loneliness ultimately led to the attainment of the highest position in his country and international admiration, respect, and moral influence.

It was lonely when things did not at first go the way George Washington Carver planned after he had advised the people to plant peanuts following the boll weevil attack on cotton in the southern United States. That sense of loneliness motivated him to experiment with the peanut, eventually producing a host of products which eventually brought economic prosperity to the people.

As a pastor, church leader, parent, manager, or leader in any field of endeavour-the loneliness of leadership. For weeping may endure for a night but joy comes in the morning. Use it as an opportunity for deep thought, research, growth, and development. The world will eventually benefit from the results that God will produce in you through the anguish of loneliness.

Henry David Thoreau, American philosopher and writer, summarize loneliness beautifully and succinctly:

I love to be alone. I never found the companion that was so companionable as solitude. We are, for the most part, more lonely when we go abroad among men than when we stay in our chambers. A man thinking or working is always alone; let him be where he will. Henry David Thoreau (1817 – 1862)

The loneliness of solitude is a leader's opportunity for retooling through reflection, meditation, prayer, and rest. Constant involvement in the thick and drive of life with the madding crowd swirling all-around can blunt the leader's keen edge, blur his vision, dissipate his energy and dampen his passion.

Loneliness is not an occasion for suicide but for self-examination and realignment with reality. Let the thoughts and feelings aroused in being alone awaken a search for God's' presence and purpose. Loneliness is a call from God to seek him who is the way, the truth, and the life. In finding him, we find meaning and fulfilment. Nathanael was lonely as he was seeking the face of God under the fig tree, but Jesus saw him and called him to be one of his apostles.

The quiet desperation experienced in loneliness will cause you to depend on God alone. He is your companion and never-failing friend when all others have forsaken you. Jesus himself

125

declared, "I will never leave you nor forsake you." He even told his disciples even as he gave them his last command, "Lo, I am with you always even unto the end of the age."

"No never alone, no never alone, He promised never to leave us, never to leave us alone."

Be of good courage, lonely leader. Remember, loneliness is not a dead-end street but the pathway to development and success. The Lord told Joshua after the death of Moses, and the mantle of leadership devolved upon him:

This book of the law shall not depart out of thy mouth; but thou shalt meditate therein day and night, that thou mayest observe to do according to all that is written therein: for then thou shalt make thy way prosperous, and then thou shalt have good success.

Have not I commanded thee? Be strong and of good courage; be not afraid, neither be thou dismayed: for the LORD thy God is with thee whithersoever thou goest.

I am suggesting an assignment for all leaders. Knowing the loneliness of leadership yourself find another leader with whom you can empathize. Listen to his heartbeat and share yours with him. Help him to carry some of his burdens even as he helps you to carry yours. Share with him what you have *learned in your loneliness and learn from him as well for according to John Donne, "No man is an island."*

Lonely people need friends. The best friend of a lonely leader is another lonely leader. Rather than be frustrated by loneliness, use it constructively, and it will pay dividends."

The Doer

A wise man once said that "A vision without a plan is just a dream. A plan without a vision is just drudgery. But a plan can change the world." So now we have come to the most challenging part. This is where many people miss greatness. Here is where thinkers and visionaries usually matriculate into extraordinary people with extraordinary plans. Doers are people who roll up their sleeves and are willing to get dirty. They knew that without a plan, the vision would never get done. The Bible tells us in James 1:22 (NKJV), "But be doers of the word, and not hearers only, deceiving yourselves." In other words, after hearing, one must conclude that action is needed to accomplish the task. *Doers know how to make it through the stage of infatuation, and turn the vision into a reality.* You can always tell when a Youth Leader has gotten beyond thoughts and vision and on to the doing phase because you will see results. Doers get results when others are still stuck in the first two phases.

As the visionary of your youth ministry, you have to be able to see beyond the five people attending youth meetings. Plan your programs to have more people. See things bigger than they truly are. Be strategic, be intentional, and be careful not to limit yourself and God. Plan big but be realistic at the same time.

Youth Leaders, you will have lonely days. You will have days when only you alone turn up for an event, meeting or service. You are expected to be the first to show up and the last one to leave. It's your vision that makes the youth ministry grow and develop into a place of maturity. Many are the responsibilities of a Youth Leader, and a clear vision is one of them. It is the Youth Leader's responsibility to develop a vision and mission statement for the youth ministry. After doing so, you should periodically revisit your vision and keep it alive. This will allow you to maintain desired progress and keep the ministry on track. These are relevant and important responsibilities of Youth Leadership.

In closing, the Youth Leader is also the 'point man'. According to the Free Online Dictionary, "A *point man* is a soldier who is assigned to a position, some distance ahead of a patrol as a lookout; a man who has a crucial, often hazardous role in the forefront of an enterprise. "The second definition particularly applies to leaders in general because leaders are point people at the forefront of an organization. They occupy an upfront position ahead of the rest. They do the reconnoitring. They check out the way forward for obstacles to the progress of the mission and look out for danger. They do the feasibility studies to determine the wisdom of moving in a particular direction. Such a role arouses a sense of loneliness in the leader. Like the Canadian goose leading the flock, he bears the brunt of the wind and breaks its force so that his companions can conserve their energy and progress can be made with reduced effort.

While others are impelled by the urgent and the immediate, the leader is compelled by his vision of the ultimate. They are satisfied with the status quo, but the leader yearns for so much more. He sees further than the average person and lives with his vision always. He eats and drinks the vision; he sleeps with the vision and dreams of the vision. While others are slumbering, he tosses, turns, and toils deep into the night. He keeps the company, church, or organization on course because he carries the vision unceasingly.

Core Values Are Foundations

"When the integrity of an organization or structure is being tested, only a strong foundation can determine a positive and lasting outcome. Youth Leadership needs strong, durable and purpose-driven individuals who will stand on values that will survive cultural storms and turmoil." – Leroy Hutchinson

I was fifteen and enjoyed the idea of having my cell phone, so you can imagine my youthful exuberance. On many occasions, I had overstayed my welcome on my mother's phone and had to give her the bad news about the expiration of the talk time. I had to be honest with her even when I didn't know how she would react. Not telling her would be considered as stealing. I grew up knowing that stealing was wrong. My parents taught me that, and they always reminded me that it is always best to ask for something rather than to steal it. That, to me, was a core value, and I continued to build on it. Eventually, I got tired of borrowing her phone to call my friends, and I think she was tired of lending, so she finally bought one for me. About a week after I got my phone I had an unforgettable experience.

It was during my lunch one day in high school. I went to the canteen, as this was my usual routine. It was a very hot and long day. I just wanted to get out of the crowd and go to a quiet place to rejuvenate. I ordered my meal, a small drink to go with it and was waiting patiently at the counter when one of the canteen staff handed me what I had purchased. Not noticing that I had received a bigger drink which cost more, I turned immediately and walked out of the line. As I was heading to my classroom, I finally realized that I had paid for a small drink and received a much bigger one. My *'core value'* alarm went off. I looked back and saw the crowd and the effort it would take to do this all over. My *'core value'* alarm got even louder. "Take it back Leroy!" my conscience screamed.

Feeling lazy and fatigued by the crowd and the already long line, I kept the big drink though I was not supposed to. I should have even thought of another plan. Maybe I could have paid the extra for it after the lunch break had ended, but I didn't. I just swept it under the carpet. I was dishonest and completely going against a core value.

Later that same day, my cellphone was stolen from my backpack. Sigh!!! My first question to my self was " OK, what will you say to God now." How could I condemn such a dishonest action done by someone, when I did a similar thing a few hours ago? The canteen suffered the loss of a bigger drink because I never did the right thing. Whether or not this was an act of God, I don't know. What I do know is that I learned a great deal of wisdom from it.

"I should have stood on what I believed." That was the regrettable statement that echoed in my ear for the entire day. I can't seem to forget that day. The day when I ignored my conviction, compromised on one of my core values and ended up regretting my decision. It was a teachable moment, one that I will never forget.

Foundations Matter

Bringing Burj Khalifa to life required a combination of visionary ideals, solid science and a super-strong foundation. At over 828 metres (2,716.5 feet) and more than 160 stories, Dubai's Burj Khalifa holds the record as the tallest building in the world, tallest free-standing structure in the world, the highest number of storeys in the world, the highest occupied floor in the world, highest outdoor observation deck in the world, elevator with the longest travel distance in the world, tallest service elevator in the world. I don't have to tell you that the foundation of this building had to be and still is remarkably strong.

Core values are similar to foundations. We all should know by now that building on a solid foundation will ensure the durability and strength of any organization or structure. When the integrity of an organization or structure is being tested, only a strong foundation can determine a positive and lasting outcome. Youth Leadership needs strong, durable and purpose-driven individuals who will stand on values that will survive cultural storms and turmoil. In a world where it seems like the governments and lawmakers are the final authority for morals, we now realize that it might become a slippery slope. Soon everything and everyone will have a right to do as they so desire. This is why Youth Leaders need to retain Godly values and also teach our youths to build their lives and other foundations on God and His word.

Value will Withstand

"Well! he huffed, and he puffed. He puffed, and he huffed. And he huffed, huffed, and he puffed, puffed; but he could not blow the house down. At last, he was so out of breath that he couldn't huff and he couldn't puff anymore. So he stopped to rest and thought a bit."

That was just a piece from the renowned childhood story of *"The Three Little Pigs"*. At the end of the story, the wolf was dealt with by the hard work of a practical Pig.

If ever a time we need hard-working, practical and responsible leaders, it is now. What is the essential pillar of your leadership and the youth ministry? While you are still wondering, let me just say that ***strong values are what we should be standing on continuously to ensure growth and development.*** They are unseen pillars that can withstand the test of times in our lives and ministry.

That should be your priority. Every organization needs core values, and your youth ministry is no different. Growing up in the Church as a teenager, as difficult as it was, I had always thought to myself that I wanted to live a life that will bring glory to God first. That was my core value. That was what I stood on and continue to stand on as a Christian to date.

Jesus Introduced Foundation

There were once two men, and each needed to build a house. The first man was foolish and chose to build on the sand where it was easy to access and easy to dig the foundations. In a few short weeks, he was almost finished. The second man was wise and chose to build his house on a rocky hill, where it was very hard to access and dig the foundation. He spent many months building his home. As time passed a violent storm rose upon the houses of these men. After much rain, a flood swept through the valley and the man's house that was built on sand was swept away. But the second man who had made his on the rocky hill was safe. No matter how hard it rained or how fierce the floods were, his house remained solid and immovable.

Let's ask ourselves the question. What's the foundation of our life? Are we like the foolish man, are our lives built on sand?

The story above is from the Matthew 7:24-27, where the Bible says:

"Therefore whosoever heareth these sayings of mine, and doeth them, I will liken him unto a wise man, which built his house upon a rock: and the rain descended, and the floods came, and the winds blew, and beat upon that house; and it fell not: for it was founded upon a rock.
And every one that heareth these sayings of mine, and doeth them not, shall be likened unto a foolish man, which built his house upon the sand: And the rain descended, and the floods came, and the winds blew, and beat upon that house, and it fell: and great was the fall of it."

Jesus said that whoever heard his words and obeyed Him, would be like a wise man who built on a rock. And that house could never be torn down!!! It could never be moved!

But if we only hear the wonderful words of Jesus and yet still go our way and don't do what He says, then we are like a foolish person, who builds his house on the sand!

Just think about that, who would want to build a house on a sand-dune? It sounds very foolish, doesn't it?

Perhaps the foolish man thought he was safe? His house was standing to start with, and it was cosy and warm inside, everything was going just fine. But when the floods came, he had no hope! His house fell flat and great was the fall of it.

What about our lives? When Satan brings temptations and trials to us, it may feel like a flood is battering us! In Isaiah 59:19, the Bible refers to the enemy coming in like a flood. And perhaps you've found yourself standing on the sand before. And when the flood of temptation or trial comes, you fall flat like that foolish man. But! Don't be discouraged; let's choose to be like the wise man. Who listens to what Jesus tells us in the Bible and does what he says!

And when we listen and obey Jesus what rock are we building our lives on? David in Psalms 18:2 uttered "The LORD [is] my rock, and my fortress, and my deliverer; my God, my strength, in whom I will trust." Jesus is our Rock! He is the firm foundation that we can build our lives upon. And if we obey Jesus, and everything He tells us in his word, the Bible, we have the assurance that no matter what flood beats upon us, no matter how fierce the storms of this life may get we will never fall, we will never be moved.

God wants us to build securely upon the eternal Rock, the word of God. We have been only hearers long enough. Let us now put the important lessons of Christ into practice. He who is a hearer and not a doer of the word, Christ compares to the man who built his house upon the sand. It needs only the storm of temptation to break upon such, and the foundation they supposed so secure is swept away. How great is the loss to these souls! They might have had eternal life--a life that measures with the life of God--had they built upon the firm foundation.

Who Is Watching

Hardly any research on the great Philosopher Thomas Hobbes will exclude the eventful day when little Hobbes witnessed his father doing something he taught against. At age 2 or 3 years old his father, a cleric, got in a fight in front of his own Church and then fled never to be found. He disappeared, abandoning his three children to the care of his brother. That must have affected young Thomas. Whatever was the reason for his father's actions, it is obvious that it had damaged his morale, and he was ashamed and embarrassed to the point of running away. He knew that he had overstepped a core value and was not able to live with the failures of that day, so he kept on running. When we swing and miss our values, it can cause pain that will lead to guilt and guilt that can lead to quitting.

Here Are Three Core Values Worth Building your Youth Ministry On

Prayer- *Keep an open communication with God at all times.*

Building a healthy youth ministry takes time. It doesn't happen quickly. Proverbs 19:2 says "Desire without knowledge is not good; how much more will hasty feet miss the way!" Building a healthy youth ministry takes leaders who depend on God's power. It's not just about programs and events. The most important quality for a leader in ministry is a pure heart. A heart the leader allows God to change, mould and reshape according to his will. The Youth Leader has to spend quality time in prayer to develop his or her ministry and leadership skills. I remember, at one point, I was frustrated with the condition of my youth ministry and sought the Lord for a change. He specifically instructed me to "keep on praying." Prayer has to be your number one core value.

139

When all other ways seem to be failing, prayer will never fail. Every Youth Leader should have a healthy prayer life.

It wasn't about his ability to preach, sing or pastor a large congregation but rather his prayer life. His prayer made him very popular. Jabez was a leader in his own right. The prayer he prayed is found in a historical note within a genealogy: "Jabez was more honourable than his brothers. His mother had named him Jabez, saying, 'I gave birth to him in pain.' Jabez cried out to the God of Israel, 'Oh that you would bless me and enlarge my territory! Let your hand be with me, and keep me from harm so that I will be free from pain.' And God granted his request" (1 Chronicles 4:9-10). Little is known of Jabez, other than he was a descendant of Judah, he was an honourable man, and his mother named him "Jabez" (meaning "sorrowful" or "sorrow-maker") because his had been a painful birth. In his prayer, Jabez cries out to God for protection and blessing. Using a play on words, Jabez, the "man of sorrow," asks God to keep him from that sorrow which his name both recalled and foreboded.

The prayer of Jabez had four critical points in it that we could learn from.

God's blessing- Asking God's blessing upon your life and youth ministry is of utmost importance. In the toughest of times when he needed a breakthrough, Jabez called on God. He recognized that the God of Israel is the source of all blessing, and he asked God for His grace. It is very critical that the Youth Leader has daily devotion and personal time with God for the furtherance and benefit of his or her ministry.

Expansion of territory- This is the cry of many Youth Leaders but also where many have failed. I believe we all want to see growth and expansion in all areas of our lives, but how do we accomplish this kind of increase? Well, my friends, Jabez, prayed for victory and prosperity in all his endeavours and that an increase would mark his life. Prayer will propel us into God's will. I'm not saying that every time we pray, God will give us an increase; instead, there can be no increase without prayer. In Luke 10 and verse 2, Jesus told His followers, "The harvest is plentiful, but the workers are few. Ask the Lord of the harvest, therefore, to send out workers into his harvest field." Jesus was indicating a principle here. That God is in charge of all things and whatsoever we desire from Him has to come through the act of prayer. Whatever increase you desire for your youth ministry, take it to God in prayer. He will supply.

God's hand. In other words, Jabez asked for the guidance of God and His strength to be evident in his daily existence. Praying God's hand upon our lives and ministry will give us a clear passage to be empowered and to also empower others. Ezekiel clearly remembered God's hand as he recounted in the 37th chapter of the book: "The hand of the Lord was on me, and he brought me out by the Spirit of the Lord and set me in the middle of a valley; it was full of bones." The Prophet was conscious of the fact that it was God's hand made a difference in his approach to the valley of dry bones. Our young people need guidance and God's hand upon their lives we have to be the intercessors on their behalf.

Protection from evil. Jesus taught His disciples to pray in this way: "Father in heaven, deliver us from the evil one" (Matthew 6:9, 13). Jabez looked to God in confidence as his defender, and so should you and I. Like Jabez, your prayer could save an entire generation from pain. Praying for your youth ministry is a principal core value that should be maintained at all times.

Honesty and Integrity - *Doing what is "Right" when no one is watching.*

But he refused. "With me in charge," he told her, "my master does not concern himself with anything in the house; everything he owns he has entrusted to my care. No one is greater in this house than I am. My master has withheld nothing from me except you because you are his wife. How then could I do such a wicked thing and sin against God?"

That was the reply from 17 years old Joseph in Genesis 39. The story is set in the household of a rich Egyptian man, Potiphar, who owned many slaves. One of these was the Hebrew young man Joseph, a man of unusual ability who had been placed in control of Potiphar's large estate and household. Potiphar's wife had no children and did not seem to love her husband. In short, she had no purpose. Rich, bored and idle, she became obsessed with Joseph.

As far as the narrator was concerned, this was a deliberate attempt by a woman to use her sexual and social power to dominate a man, and as such, it was definitely a bad thing.

Joseph was in a delicate situation. He had to either offend the wife or betray her husband. He judged that the former was less dangerous and repulsed the woman.

God was watching him, although he was miles away from his parents in Egypt. In the Joseph story, good things happen to bad people, and bad things turn out to be good things by misadventure.

Thankfulness - *Giving thanks to God at all times for all things, no matter how small they are.*

"A proud man is seldom a grateful man, for he never thinks he gets as much as he deserves", says Henry Ward Beecher. The psalmist David was well known for his continuous gratitude towards God. Having a heart of thanksgiving is ultimately a blessing in and of itself. I have come to realize that too.

The Apostle Paul in 1 Thessalonians 5:18 reminds us, "In everything give thanks: for this is the will of God in Christ Jesus concerning you." Teach young people to be grateful in all situations. Let us try to see the positive in most things and quit complaining about everything. "Gratitude can transform common days into thanksgivings, turn routine jobs into joy, and change ordinary opportunities into blessings", William Arthur Ward wrote.

In an article by **David Mathis,** Executive Editor, desiringGod.org, he recited, "Only in Jesus, the paragon of creaturely appreciation, are we able to become the kind of persistently thankful people God created us to be and fulfil the human destiny of thanksgiving. For the

Christian, with both feet standing firmly in the good news of Jesus, there are possibilities for a true thanksgiving which we otherwise would never know."

Gospel Artist Jermaine Edwards said, "Jesus first, everything comes after."

With Christ as the rock of our salvation, we will be victorious. He is our firm foundation. If we build and maintain our lives and youth ministry on Him and his values, we will never be put to shame.

7

Speak The Same Language Pay Attention; They Need Us

"No one asked us if we wanted to be young first; therefore being a youth is not an option. It is a way of life."– Leroy Hutchinson

The Language Barrier

One of the most sensitive challenges for the Youth Leader is the ability to communicate with their youths. The fact that someone has been appointed to the office of a Youth Leader, it doesn't mean they have the skillsets to communicate with youths. Communication, as we know, is critical in every stage of life and at all levels of relationships. If one cannot understand the other; then one cannot cooperate and coexist. Many Youth Ministry Leaders often find themselves in a constrained area as a result of their inability to properly communicate in a way that youths can understand. Whenever this happens, it can be very chaotic.

I have heard parents on numerous occasions seeking help with their teenaged boys and girls. There is a desperate need for a breaking down of the language barrier that exists between the two generations. Language barriers can become the chief destroyers of communication. In such a predicament, the Youth Leader has to find what I called a common ground, something that will demonstrate the essential message. You cannot compete with all the other messages being yelled at them. Find a way to get closer to them and be more effective.

Roberta Michnick Golinkoff, Ph.D., is a noted infant language researcher and co-author of the book *How Babies Talk: The Magic and Mystery of Language in the First Three Years of Life*. Roberta believes that "Language learning begins in the womb." I agree. Parents have a unique opportunity and the ability to communicate with babies in the womb by singing and projecting vocal levels, creating an early connection with infants that could result in significant bonding after birth. This is a fascinating truth that has been proven by researchers over the years and can still be acted upon by those who still have an interest in communicating with youths, even during the teenage and young adult stages.

There are many features on my car radio that I'm still unable to access. That's because the language on the stereo system is in Japanese. Simply put, I don't speak Japanese, but the car was made in Japan. I have been able to study the buttons based on what happens when I click them. I may not be able to read the language, but I certainly know what will happen if I select a feature. Like my stereo and I, it would be unrealistic to ask a Youth Leader to learn every language. Youth Leaders are not expected to speak the same language in the beginning, but can eventually learn and be able to know what feature to tap into and what to avoid.

In a football match between teams such as France and Spain for example, there may be a huge language barrier with both teams having distinct independent and official languages. The only reason these two teams can successfully play a game is based on principles; principles that govern the game and not the languages. They are unable to understand each other except they know the opposite language; hence, the goal here is to put the ball into the opposing team's net. How often do teams and individuals play sports without speaking the same language? Sport has become a universal language, not words.

The Youth Leader's responsibility is to observe and learn how to communicate effectively with each person in the Youth Ministry. Some youths may not even speak as fluently as others do. Some may not even speak at all. They would instead communicate using technology and social media, but the leader has to be able to keep up. There is no excuse for not being able to communicate. That is how serious it as it relates to effective communication and your youth ministry. Get with the program. Get on the necessary social media platforms like WhatsApp, Facebook, email or simply text messaging, not for your reasons sometimes but for the sake of those you want to empower. We must be at the right place waiting for them, to reach them and overcome the language barrier.

Look At Us Now

How we communicate with today's generation will propel us into successful Youth Leadership and mature youth ministries. We dare not forget how we passed through those stages of communication as youths, so we can be who we are today. Someone had to speak to us, beseech us and even oppose us, all in an effort to get us to understand what was being communicated. The offices, career, bills, cars, degrees, houses, marriage, parenthood, pulpits, maturity, responsibilities and the corporate world are just a view of the various aspects that mark adulthood and what it entails. They all seem to remind us of where we are, how hard we have worked, the pitfalls, the successes and how far we have come as grownups. Some of us have been through uproars, turmoil, disasters and terrible times in the journey to adulthood.

As life gave us its best shot, we somehow managed to make it out alive. Yet when we look around, there are still playgrounds with children, classrooms packed with teens, soccer fields, youth clubs, youth ministries and a wide range of youthful exuberance staring us in the face. We cannot escape youth internally and externally. For many of us adults, it is confusing. As time changes, the older practices are gone out the door and in come the new. Cultures altered and this generation standing before us breathes disaster. A tablet that is hard to swallow; I would call it. We hope against hope that our children and their children will find a sense of peace in a cold and dark world. We pray that God will somehow send help, but may I tell you, you are the help that you have been waiting for.

The 21st century's youths have specific needs. It is as if they have come from different dynasties. Unlike the previous generation, there is no Michael Jackson, Elvis Presley, Beatles, or Bob Marley concerts. No funky music, Afro hairstyles and legged fitted clothes as were the leading trends. Instead, we look around us, and we see a social media era with information at the tip of our fingers. As adults, we can be very forgetful. How many of us have forgotten that being young played a part in who we are today? Being a youth is not an option. It is a way and a stage of life. You can't choose to be born as an adult. This reminds me of the movie I watched some years ago call Benjamin Button. He was born under unusual circumstances; Benjamin Button played by actor (Brad Pitt) springs into being as an elderly man in a New Orleans nursing home and then ages in reverse. Well sorry to say we don't age in reverse in real life. There is a period of development that we all must go through. Whether we want to admit it or not, the stages of youth are psychologically challenging phases of the human life cycle. These stages were designed initially by God Himself for a reason and should not be ignored by those who have been entrusted to lead his young people. As Youth Leaders we must understand how to relate to the specific needs of youths in the given areas that we serve, and to do this, we must first look at particular definitions and what determines who youths are.

Youth Defined

According to the United Nations, "Youth is best understood as a period of transition from the dependence of childhood to adulthood's independence. This is why, as a category, youth is more fluid than other fixed age-groups. Yet, age is the easiest way to define this group, particularly concerning education and employment, because 'youth' is often referred to as persons between the ages of leaving required education, and finding their first job. Definition of youth perhaps changes with circumstances, especially with the changes in demographic, financial, economic and socio-cultural settings; however, the meaning that uses 15- 24 age cohort as youth reasonably serves its statistical purposes for assessing the needs of the young people and providing guidelines for youth development."

We find ourselves sometimes struggling to understand individuals at this age. Be it your child or someone else's, the stages of a youth's life can be very confusing and challenging. Take a look at these articles posted on January 7, 2013, by Janelle Stewart, Michigan State University Extension as we explore the ages and stages of youth development. This article focuses on age 6-8, 9-11, 12-14, 15-17 and 18-19. I found this information very helpful, and it improved my approach to working with youths as a Youth Leader. This will also assist you in planning, strategizing and executing the different programs and activities for the respective age ranges within your youth ministry.

"Understanding the different stages of youth development supports youth programming efforts as it encourages relationship building between youth and adult volunteers. In building relationships with youth, it is vital to understand the development of the child. Not all children grow at the same pace, but they share many common characteristics of growth and development throughout their life. This article introduces the topic and examines the implications of working with youth ages 6 to 8 years old.

Within each age groupings, growth and development are typically studied through four major areas of development: physical, social, emotional and intellectual. Physical development refers to the growth of the body and the development of motor skills. Social development is the interaction between children and their ability to function in social settings. Emotional development looks at how youth handle their feelings and express them. Finally, intellectual development is all about how individuals learn.

Early elementary youth (ages 6 to 8) are typically going through the following growth and development processes:

Physical

- They are mastering physical skills
- They have better control of large muscles than small muscles

Social

- They are learning how to be friends and may have several best friends at one time
- They are becoming more aware of peers and their opinions
- They are family-oriented

Emotional

- They see fairness as being nice to others so others will be nice to them
- They seek parental/adult approval
- They tend to behave in ways to avoid punishment

Intellectual

- They base their thinking in reality and accuracy
- They are learning to sort things into categories
- They are beginning to develop a sense of cause and effect

When working with children in the age range of 6 to 8, a volunteer, parent, educator or youth development expert must keep the following implications in mind:

Physical

- Their craft projects could end up messy
- Their activities need to be just that – active

- Plan activities that practice both small muscles and large ones
- Work on skills that can be completed successfully by beginners

Social

- Small group activities are best
- Break them into groups in order to encourage them to interact with different children
- They need a lot of praise as they are seeking adult approval
- They need to accept the beliefs and values of parents

Emotional

- Focus on cooperative games in which every child wins
- Find ways to have more success than failures
- Be available to discuss fears and other issues important to them, no matter how small

Intellectual

- Reading to a child in this age group is effective and enjoyed

- Help them predict answers to their questions – successes
- Be flexible – provide a variety of activities
- Role-playing and skits are often a popular way to learn and interact
- Regardless of their age, all youth and adults have basic needs that programs should consider and provide opportunities to develop. All youth and adults need:
- To experience a positive self-concept
- To experience success in what they attempt to do
- To become increasingly independent
- To be accepted by people of different ages – peers as well as those in authority
- To give and receive affection
- To experience adventure

As we move into the 9- to 11-year-old age bracket, the youth's physical development is starting to move to the forefront. They will experience growth spurts at different rates that move them towards adolescence. Typically girls will begin to grow and mature faster than boys during this period.

Providing active learning experiences is helpful during this time. Hands-on events or activities where they are up and moving – not limited only to sitting and listening

– is best. Youth at this age are also developing a more competitive nature between boys and girls. Try to avoid activities that create competition between gender groups. Choose activities that mix boys and girls in a group on an even playing field.

9 to 11-year-olds are developing in the following ways, outlined below:

Physical

- They experience a steady increase in large muscle development, strength, balance and coordination
- They are very active, with a lot of energy
- There will be different maturation rates between the sexes; girls will tend to mature faster than boys
- They will experience an increase in small muscle coordination

Social

- They generally see adults as authority
- They follow rules out of respect for authority
- They are loyal to groups, clubs, gangs, etc.
- They enjoy code languages and passwords
- They identify with individuals of the same gender
- They prefer to work in groups in cooperative activities

- They approach solving problems with a negotiating style, compromising with peers

Emotional

- They are accepting parent/family beliefs
- They admire and imitate older youth
- They are developing decision-making skills
- They are beginning to question authority
- They need involvement with a caring adult
- They find comparisons with others difficult to process

Intellectual

- Their academic abilities vary greatly
- They have an increased attention span, but many have interests which change rapidly
- They are learning to use good judgment
- They judge ideas in absolutes, right or wrong not much tolerance for a middle ground
- They have interests in collections and hobbies

The implications of developing programs or interacting with 9- to 11-year-olds:

Physical

- Plan activities that allow them to move about

- Vary activities – don't rely solely on sports, general physical activities are important as well
- Avoid competitions between genders

Social

- Clarify and enforce reasonable limits
- Plan plenty of time to be with individuals from their same gender
- Group activities are important

Emotional

- Provide correction quietly – one-on-one
- Give positive feedback and look for successes
- Avoid generalized praise
- Be present at group activities, be visible but be in the background
- Provide safety net of an adult that will maintain boundaries

Intellectual

- Youth in this age bracket still very much enjoy "hands-on" activities
- Help youth form groups/clubs with common interests or hobbies

- Vary the activities offered to engage rapidly changing interests

A room full of young teens can be energizing or terrifying to youth workers or volunteers. Young teens, ages 12 to 14, are at the prime age to engage them in leadership roles and give them a voice in decision making. Looking at Michigan State University Extension's 4-H Guiding Principles shows the impact of having youth actively engaged in their development.

Under this principle, youth are considered participants – rather than recipients – in the learning process; youth in this age bracket are at a wonderful age to begin exploring these principles. Youth ages 12 to 14 want to feel ownership for projects; involving them in the planning results in buy-in and commitment from them.

Much like the two previous articles looking at the characteristics and implications of working with 6- to 8-year-olds and 9- to 11-year-olds, this article considers 12- to 14-year-olds' physical, social, emotional and intellectual development.

Youth in the age range of 12 to 14 are developing in the following ways:

Physical

- They exhibit a wide range of sexual maturity and growth patterns between genders and within gender groups
- They experience rapid changes in physical appearance
- Changes in their appearance can occur at different rates, causing great concern

Social

- They are interested in activities involving individuals of the opposite sex
- They are looking more to peers than parents
- They seek acceptance and trust
- They tend to reject ready-made solutions from adults in favour of their own
- They question authority and family values

Emotional

- They compare themselves to others
- They are concerned about physical development
- They see themselves as always centre stage

- They are concerned about social graces, friends, being liked, etc.
- They strive for independence, yet want and need adult approval
- They seek privacy

Intellectual

- They find justice and equality to be important issues
- They are developing skills in the use of logic
- They can solve problems that have more than one variable
- They are ready for in-depth, long-term experiences
- They want to explore the world beyond their own community

Implications for working with this age group:

Physical

- Provide honest information for the sexual questions and issues they have
- Plan activities that are not weighted toward physical powers
- Be patient with grooming behaviours that may seem excessive

Social

- Provide activities to be with the opposite sex in healthy ways, planning groups, parties, fundraising, etc.
- Encourage involvement in teen councils and planning boards
- Find time to talk with them individually to help them work through problems or discuss issues

Emotional

- Plan activities that do not compare one youth with another
- Avoid singling them out in front of others
- Provide opportunities to learn skills

Intellectual

- Provide opportunities to ask and question ways of doing things
- Plan activities that require some length of time to complete
- Ask questions to encourage predicting and problem-solving
- Let them serve as assistants
- Offer more complex games

In working with this age bracket, adults must have open communication with them! They are growing both physically and emotionally at rapid paces and need individuals who will be open and honest with them. This is the age bracket many adults shy away from because of tweens' need to pull away from an adult and establish independence. Stay with the tween; get to know them as an individual and learn to understand and appreciate them for who they are, not just as part of the group.

Teenagers are a group of individuals who are full of life, enthusiasm, energy and the feeling that they can do anything. They feel as if they can conquer the world – what's more is that they feel they are ready to. They are impressionable where physical appearance is concerned and can be easily misguided by advertising and the emphasis our society places on physical appearance. With this age group, we need to be open to answering questions and must keep the lines of communication open.

Much like the three previous articles that examined the characteristics and implications of working with 6- to 8-year-olds, 9- to 11-year-olds and 12- to 14-year-olds, this article examines the physical, social, emotional and intellectual development of youth ages 15 to 17.

Youth in the age range of 15 to 17 are developing in the following ways:

Physical

- They are concerned about body image
- They exhibit a small range in size and maturity among peers
- They tend to have realistic views of limits to which their body can be tested

Social

- They search for intimacy, tend to endeavour
- They make commitments
- They desire respect
- They want adult leadership roles
- They can commit to following through

Emotional

- They are beginning to accept and enjoy their own uniqueness but still seek approval from peer groups

- They look for the confidence of others in their decisions
- They can see self from the viewpoint of others
- They take fewer risks
- They can initiate and carry out their own tasks without the supervision of others
- They search for career possibilities

Intellectual

- They are mastering abstract thinking
- They enjoy demonstrating acquired knowledge
- They can consider many perspectives of a given issue
- They will lose patience with meaningless activity

The implications of working with youth 15 to 17-year-olds:

Physical

- Provide experiences around body image, etiquette, grooming, etc.
- Avoid comments that criticize or compare stature, size or shape at all costs

Social

- Provide activities to explore the job market, careers, etc.
- Provide opportunities for them to plan their own programs
- Provide opportunities to talk about their own beliefs
- Involve them as spokespersons for issues, programs, etc.

Emotional

- Plan activities that allow teens to try different roles
- Be willing to be wrong; this age group won't put you on a pedestal

Intellectual

- Involve them in carrying out plans
- Involve them in advisory groups, decision making groups
- Offer vocational/career exploration activities
- Individuals in this age may have a declining interest in past activities, but offering them an

opportunity to be a leader, tapping into their energy, skills and knowledge will allow you to build a leader in them, but also keep them interested in positive programs that have and will facilitate their development.

The final age bracket in this series will examine the older teens: 18- to 19-year-olds, who much prefer to be called "young adults." This is the age where physically, the growth and development has slowed. Still, socially and emotionally, they are transitioning from what has been somewhat of a routine and protective environment to the unknown.

Much like the four previous articles looking at the characteristics and implications of working with 6- to 8-year-olds, 9- to 11-year-olds, 12- to 14-year-olds and 15- to 17-year-olds; we will be looking at the physical, social, emotional and intellectual development of 18- to 19-year-olds.

Young adults ages 18 to 19 are developing in the following ways:

Physical

- Their growth has tapered off
- They are not as preoccupied with body changes

- They have adult bodies but are not always prepared entirely for adulthood

Social

- They value committed relationships
- They're looking for more adult social settings, looking at moving on from "teen" activities
- They make their own decisions
- They want support from adults, but only in guidance
- They are developing community consciousness

Emotional

- Previous activities have lost their appeal
- They enjoy looking back on their achievements
- They look for recognition in bigger picture accomplishments
- They feel as if they have reached the stage of full maturity
- They expect others to treat them as if they are "fully" grown

Intellectual

- They're making future plans
- They're setting long-term goals

- They make their own schedule, plans, etc.

Implications of working with youth 18 to 19-year-olds:

Physical

- Avoid comments that criticize or compare stature, size, or shape
- Encourage healthy activities that provide exercise but not a competition

Social

- Provide activities that are just for older teens, young adults
- Provide opportunities for them to plan, facilitate and carry out their own programs
- Involve them as spokesperson around reflecting on their involvement/accomplishments

Emotional

- Provide them with next step opportunities to stay involved
- Give them opportunities to "try" on the "adult hat."
- Provide opportunities for learners to talk about their own beliefs

Intellectual

- Involve them in planning and carrying out programs, allow them to teach or be the leaders
- Involve them in advisory groups, decision making groups, giving them major roles
- Offer vocational/career exploration activities
- Plan group time where learners can discuss ideas and concepts
- As adults support youth in moving on to the next step in their lives, remember that every child is unique. Regardless of their age, all youth have basic needs that adults and youth development programs should support:
  o To experience a positive self-concept
  o To experience success in what they attempt to do
  o To become increasingly independent
  o To be accepted by people of different ages – peers as well as those in authority
  o To give and receive affection
  o To experience adventure

Here is a Sample Job Description for the Youth Leader prepared by Minister Megan Hylton (Church of God of Prophecy, Jamaica).

Purpose - The Youth Leader shall be responsible for the general oversight of ministry to youths ages 12- 40. He/she must minister to the needs of teens and young adults, leading them to spiritual commitment and discipline that will result in spiritual maturity. The Youth Leader's position exists to administer, develop and implement teens and young adult ministries and programs designed to meet the spiritual, social and emotional needs of both groups. (Youth Ministries Resource Manual, pgs. 21)

Responsibilities: Consider, Coordinate, Care, Communicate

- **Consider**: developing ministry and programs that will accomplish the following:
- Evangelize and disciple youth and young adults.
- Teach youths how to worship and fellowship
- Equip youth for life changes.
- Minister to young people at their age and spiritual level.

- Seek out and develop young leaders.
- Recruit and train leaders who have a passion for shepherding and disciplining youths.
- Communicate a vision for youth ministry that is Christ centred and relational.
- Monitor the accomplishment of the goals and objectives of the ministry.

Coordinate: Statistics show that we lose young people during some traditional stages in life; between teens and young adult; between young adult and young married, etc. **It is the responsibility of the youth minister to ensure that programs are in place to provide a smooth transition from one age range to the next, as well as from one spiritual level to the next. The transition can be a challenging time - youth need guidance.**

- **Care**: The Youth Leader is called into a caring relationship with young people. This expression of care must find its origin in the love and care that God the Father has for us. The love of God is the thing that motivates the young leader to minister to young people.

- **Communicate**: The mark of an effective youth minister is the ability to communicate. He or she must be able to communicate the vision and the mission to the senior pastor, parents, volunteer staff etc. Communication between Youth Leader and youth regarding expectations, correction, affirmation, admiration, is also crucial.
- (Youth Ministries Resource Manual, pgs. 21-22)

Other Responsibilities:

- Work with appointed youth coordinators to appoint an executive committee and select volunteer workers for the youth department. (Persons chosen should be given the option of declining-(no) one should not be forced to serve. Workers should be capable of effectively performing the duties assigned to them.)
- Work with the coordinators and executive committee to plan a wholesome youth ministry program that ministers to the youth as a whole person. All activities, however (whether spiritual, social, sports-related etc. should be Christ-centred and aimed at winning the lost for Christ).

- Ensure that proper prayer and planning precede all Youth Ministry activities.
- Coordinate and/ or supervise Youth Ministry Services as scheduled by the local church (e.g. Sunday morning service, Sunday night Service, Weeknight Meetings etc.)
- Coordinate or the involvement of the youths in practical projects/ acts of service within the sphere of the local church and community (e.g. adopting a children's home, creating a home-work assistance program etc.)
- Promote and solicit support from youths within the local Church for the Parish and national youth ministry events (e.g. Parish Youth Ministries Retreat)
- Be a team player in mobilizing department members towards achieving the general and specific spiritual and financial goals of the local church.

Accountability
- The youth director is directly accountable to the youth coordinators and pastor/ pastoral team.

- The Youth Leader should be a team player and will work in conjunction with the pastoral team, and ministry leaders within the church.
- The Youth Leader is accountable to the parish youth director/ committee.
- The Youth Leader or designate should present a written /typed comprehensive report of the department's achievements, projects and setbacks as well as financial status at each local church business conference.
- The Youth Leader should submit a comprehensive report to the Parish Youth Ministry Director/Committee at least once per quarter.
- Attend meetings/seminars called by Parish and/or National Directors.
- Points to Remember:
- The youth ministry director should be an example to the believers in:
- -word and deed
- -general conduct
- -dress/attire and personal hygiene
- -faithfulness in tithing and free-will offerings
- -active participation in church worship services and other activities

- -motivating youth to grow and serve as members and representatives of the kingdom of God.

I do hope the information in this chapter will give readers a motivation to want to know about youths and their development. While it is a lot to digest, it is very much relevant to and helpful. I often time believe we criticize that which we cannot understand. Having a better and more rounded understanding of the stages of youth will provide a certain level of confidence in your approach as a Youth Leader.

STEP 3

ATTITUDES YOU NEED

8

Delegate- Give Them a Chance, Trust Them Enough

"Your willingness to delegate will have to surpass your eagerness to be the *"Super"* Youth Leader who takes on all the work. Delegating does not mean that you are relinquishing your responsibilities. It means you are dissecting the tasks into smaller portions, but you are still the person in charge of the bigger picture and by extension, the outcome."–
Leroy Hutchinson

In my first year serving as the newly appointed Youth Leader, I was a little overzealous and confident. Ok, let me rephrase, it was more than a few, it was a whole lot. The passion to serve was high. The pleasure of knowing that I had been allowed to impact even a small portion of my generation was overwhelming. Whatever resided in me began to surface, and that made me feel invincible. This feeling of euphoria and invincibility is quite familiar for young leaders. Some would still say I act that way even today; nevertheless, I call it excitement for the task.

It wasn't really my game plan; it was just all I had in the beginning, so that led me to try taking on every task without seeking assistance from my youths or considering building a capable committee. Little did I know that this was going to catch up on me later, on my journey. I had a weakness, and that was my inability to delegate.

Leading a youth ministry is never a walk in the park. From personal experience, I can tell you that it can be exhausting. I learned this the hard way. I tried to do everything, not because I wanted to, but when I asked my youths, they would say no, mostly due to fear. For those who said yes, they either never started or left the task incomplete resulting in me having to do it myself.

This happened for a while, but then it became draining. It was then I realized that I needed to stop taking no for an answer and deliberately work on delegating duties and building a capable team. There were many things that I could have transferred to someone else. Doing that would have afforded me more time to focus on other areas that needed my attention. The role of a Youth Leader is not necessarily to do everything for youths but to find and develop youths by making them responsible for specific tasks.

Don't Underestimate Your Youths

Developing your youth ministry will require a level of trust on your part. There comes a time when you will have to share the tasks just as you have shared the vision. Underestimating the potential of those around you will not give the level of maturity you need; instead, it will only cause you to experience unnecessary pressure and eventually, you will be exhausted. Your willingness to delegate will have to surpass your eagerness to be the *"Super"* Youth Leader who takes on all the work. Delegating does not mean you are relinquishing your responsibilities. It means you are dissecting the tasks into smaller portions, but you are still the person in charge of the bigger picture and by extension, the outcome. "You can delegate authority, but you cannot delegate responsibility," says Byron Dorgan. The buck stops at you, but it doesn't necessarily have to be done by you, especially when there are capable people around you.

If your vision for your youth ministry can only be accomplished by you, then it probably wasn't big enough in the first place. Invite your youths to come and take part in the vision. After all, they are a part of the vision. Allow them to lead projects and take on manageable matters. Trust them enough to lead at some point. It was Nelson Mandela who said" Lead from the back and let others believe they are in front." I am in total agreement with that statement. Whenever we do this, we present an opportunity for them to see the hidden gifts within and also allow them to have the same confidence in themselves. Everybody wins whenever a Youth Leader delegates duties within the youth ministry. Here are ten (10) reasons why Youth Leaders will always benefit from delegating tasks to others around them and reap success.

- Delegating *Presents* an opportunity to focus on new tasks.
- Delegating *Uncovers* unrealized tasks.
- Delegating *Divides* the tasks.
- Delegating creates *Support*.

- Delegating creates *Flexibility.*
- Delegating highlights *Others.*
- Delegating eliminates *Insecurity.*
- Delegating *Utilizes* everyone.
- Delegating *Reinforces* authority.
- Delegating affords *Rest.*

Young Followers Today, Adult Leaders Tomorrow

There is an expression that the Church is always one generation away from extinction or extermination. Of course, I have never bought into this philosophy, but I believe, however, that we can minimize such reflection by giving youths a chance to realize their own contribution to the development of the Church or whichever organization they are a part of. Paul Polman had the same idea when he said, "Leadership is not just about giving energy; it's unleashing other people's energy." Whenever we delegate, it unleashes them into what they didn't even know they had in the first place.

Whenever I am appointed leader for a committee, my immediate plan was to find my replacement as soon as possible. I begin looking for someone I can recommend for the job should I resign tomorrow and this doesn't mean I'm not enjoying the position. This not a lack of interest in the position, but rather high regard for vision hence the effort to identify a capable successor. "Success, without a successor, is no success", wrote John Maxwell. I do this to challenge both myself and those I'm leading. I call it working my way out of a job, but this cannot happen without an attitude to delegate tasks and duties to others and to express the belief that they will deliver.

If at the end of your tenure as a Youth Leader you cannot find someone to continue the vision and the work in the youth ministry, or even to submit a name to a superior, then this means you have failed as a leader. I know it sounds hard but consider my argument. The earlier you start to delegate, the better you will be able to see the potential leaders among your youth group. Youth Leaders have to face the fact that we can't do everything. We should never try to do it alone unless there is no other option. Many youths are eagerly waiting to be drafted into the bigger vision. They should not be kept waiting for too long because the youth of today are the leaders of tomorrow. With this truth in mind, it should be self-evident that Youth Leaders ought to take their commitment to youth ministry seriously. If the youth are the leaders of tomorrow, then they need to be a priority today.

Young people are at times hesitant to believe that they can handle a task effectively as teens or young adults. There are times when they wonder if they can live as a victorious Christian in today's world. Others conclude that teenagers have no interest in the things of God, they only think about movie stars, the latest musical sensation, clothes, gadgets and the opposite sex. Perhaps we might even be inclined to ask, "What real value can young people be to the church today?" What we will find is that Youth Leaders who take care of their youth ministry and value them will be rewarded now and in the future.

Like the Apostle Paul stood up for young Timothy and entrusted him the leadership of the Church at Ephesus, we have to believe in the youths we are leading. Encourage them not to allow anyone to push them out of God's kingdom. The Apostle Paul encouraged Timothy when he wrote, "Let no man despise thy youth…" (1 Timothy 4:12-16).

In 2 Timothy 4:1-5 Paul spoke strongly yet again to Timothy when he said "In the presence of God and of Christ Jesus, who will judge the living and the dead, and in view of his appearing and his kingdom, I give you this charge: [2]*Preach the word*; be *prepared* in season and out of season; *correct, rebuke and encourage*—with great patience and careful instruction. [3] For the time will come when people will not put up with sound doctrine. Instead, to suit their own desires, they will gather around them a great number of teachers to say what their itching ears want to hear. ⁴They will turn their ears away from the truth and turn aside to myths. ⁵*But you, keep your* head in all situations, *endure hardship*, do the work of an evangelist, *discharge* all the duties of your ministry."

Paul demonstrated a level of confidence in young Timothy that I believe all Youth Leaders can observe and learn from. He fought to keep Timothy in the ministry and continuously reminded him that quitting was not an option despite his age. This seems to be a frequent recurrence in the scriptures as we often see God use people of young ages in the Bible to carry out his will. Mary, the mother of Jesus, was but a teenager when she conceived, David was only a young man when he became a giant slayer, and Samuel the prophet was only a young boy when God called him to minister in the tabernacle. God is still working in the hearts of teenagers and young adults today. Youth Leaders, I urge you to take them on mission trips, locally and internationally, in communities, children's homes, or anywhere you find an opportunity to demonstrate God's love through meeting people's needs. Expose them to new cultures, and I promise you they will not forget the adventure. Their enthusiasm and excitement as they are involved in the life and work of the church will have a positive aspect on other members, making church an even more joyful place to be. They will remember that in the future, and share those kinds of experiences with others. Youths are important and are the leaders of tomorrow. So ensure that you create an environment which welcomes youth, and encourages them to part take in the vision.

Let Them Triumph Without You

Once in the summer, my youth ministry hosted a talent completion that we entitled "My go hard or go home." It was a huge and exciting event. It lasted over five weeks, and it grew each Friday night. In the beginning, we had many youths from the community auditioning for the final round of ten (10). The event grew rapidly, and each night we had an influx of young people participating in dancing, singing, poetry and other areas of creative arts from both inside and outside the youth ministry. The competition finally narrowed down to only three contestants and the date for the final night was announced with extreme anticipation.

Unfortunately, I did not check my schedule before announcing the date of the finals, so there was now a clash with a weekend retreat that had already confirmed me to be the guest speaker. I thought long and hard about it when I found out, but I told the committee of youths that I would go to the retreat and they would just have to manage the final night without me. I told them I knew they could do it.

The stage was set, and it was the final night of excitement. I called a few times to ensure that everything was in place, but that's as much as I could have done. Of course, I felt terrible that I had to leave them, but at the end of the night the person I left in charge called and said, "Leroy, it was a success and the best night of the entire competition!" I was delighted to know that the best night they had was on a night that I was absent. Sheryl Sandberg says, "Leadership is about making others better as a result of your presence and making sure that impact lasts in your absence." That is precisely what happened on that final night.

Delegate and let them triumph on their own so that your youths can recognize that youth ministry does not revolve around the Youth Leader or any one person for that matter. It should be the joy of your heart when great things can happen, even when you, the Youth Leader, is absent. They have to learn how to take charge without you being there. That's exactly what I said to one of my board members when I got a phone call about the ministry vehicle being non- functional. I was on a mission trip in Cape Town, South Africa at the time, so I could do nothing about it even if I wanted to. In my response, I told him, "Well, I'm not there, so you will have to fix the problem because you are presently in charge."In the end, he fixed the problem, the vehicle was fully functional, and the whole matter of delegating prevailed once again.

AIESEC, the world's largest non-profit youth-run organization wrote "To develop leaders, companies need to give people the space to try and the responsibility to solve their problems in order to be more innovative and have higher emotional intelligence. If companies want more innovation and for their talent to take ownership for their work, the communication structure of the company cannot be a reflection of the hierarchy structure: everyone must be free to input."

There is always something to gain when those we lead can still triumph in our absence as a result of us trusting them to do so. I have thought about ten (10) positive outcomes on their part. Take a look and see how this could help you when allowing them to lead occasionally.

- They develop *Confidence.*
- They build *Self-esteem.*

- They **Represent** what they believe.
- They nurture unseen **Gifts**.
- They **Realize** that you are limited.
- They gain **Independence**.
- They **Contribute** to the big picture.
- They **Overcome** fear.
- They **Serve** others.
- They **Appreciate** small victories.

A lot has been said in this chapter about delegating. By now, I am sure that you have grasped the importance of delegating and how much of a useful tool it is to your development in Youth Leadership. They may not always do it your way at first, but youth development takes time and patience so let them give it a try. With this in mind, you will begin to understand both the strengths and weaknesses of those you lead. Founder of United Therapeutics and Sirius, Martine Rothblatt says, "Anything worthwhile in life requires teamwork, and you cannot manage what you don't understand." That is why every Youth Leader should seek to develop the art of seeing youths for who they can become and not just who they are at present. Never withhold the opportunities to participate from them, even if they are inexperienced. "Inexperience is an asset. Embrace it."

Wendy Kopp wrote. Give them a chance; trust them to deliver.

9

F.A.R.M. (Find, Accommodate, Reach, Mentor)

"Your Youth Ministry is depending on you to be a farmer with a good attitude, one who knows how to plant, nurture and reap in due seasons. You have been given the mandate to farm, but this time it is not plants, it is young people. Sometimes it may take years before you see results because it's a different kind of crop; however, this kind of effect will last for a lifetime."- Leroy Hutchinson

The Principle

A few months ago, my daughter planted an orange seed in the front of the yard. Every day that she got the opportunity to water it, she did. There were days when we were on a rush to leave the house, and she would say "Daddy just wait for me a little please until I give my tree some water". She would do random checks to see if the tree was growing and watered it if she thought it was needed. There were also days when I had to wait patiently for her and allowed her to nurture the young tree she had sown because that is the general principle of what farming is all about. Farming can be a hard task, but every farmer knows about this one basic principle; what you sow is what you reap. Every Youth Leader should know it too. This is not only applicable to physical farming, but rather, it is a divine principle.

Your youth ministry is depending on you to be a farmer with a good attitude, one who knows how to plant, nurture and reap in due seasons. You have been given the mandate to farm, but this time it is not to farm plants or ground provisions, it is young people instead. Sometimes it may take years before you see results because it's a different kind of crop; however, this kind of effect will last for a lifetime. As the old Chinese proverb says, "If you are planning for a year, sow rice; if you are planning for a decade, plant trees; if you are planning for a lifetime, grow people."

Your efforts as a Youth Leader will not always be received positively but keep farming. Jesus himself shared a few downsides to agriculture in Matthew chapter 13 when he said "A farmer went out to sow his seeds. As he was scattering the seed, some fell along the path, and birds came and ate it up. Some fell on rocky places, where it did not have much soil. It sprang up quickly because the soil was shallow. But when the sun came up, the plants were scorched, and they withered because they had no root. Other seed fell among thorns, which grew up and choked the plants. Still, other seed fell on good soil, where it produced a crop - a hundred, sixty or thirty times what was sown."

Amidst the other theological explanations to this text, it is also evident that Jesus intended to let the crowd know that sowers will not always get the result they desire. I am sure that I have said it before, but I'll repeat it. Youth Ministry is hard work. After you have scattered your efforts, what seems like birds, the shallowness of soil and thorns may discredit your work and bring discouragement. Nevertheless, despite the challenges of the farmer in the analogy that Jesus gave, he still got a chance to reap from good soil. Your reaping is mainly dependent on where the seed falls, how it is received and what happens when its challenges come.

The oppositions you face as a Youth Leader in your ministry may be more than what you had bargained for, but the benefits are worth your time and patience. Jared Moore reminded us of this truth when she penned, "The blessings of ministry far outweigh the realities below; however, the ministry is not easy. Don't waste your time and money going to seminary or college for pastoral training if you are not prepared for the negative aspects of ministry mentioned below. Furthermore, always remember that God has called you to love His church, not merely His mature church, but His immature church as well. Moreover, a call to ministry is a call to bleed."

While plants and animals don't talk back to farmers, but people do. The products might be different, but the principles remain the same. I have observed ten (10) things about farming, that I thought I would share with you about farming lives. These principles will provide help to you as a Youth Leader in your quest to cultivate youths.

- Farming is *Risky.*

- Farming is *Time.*
- Farming is *Discipline.*
- Farming is *Investment.*
- Farming is *Faith.*
- Farming is *Balance.*
- Farming is *Decisiveness.*
- Farming is *Patience.*
- Farming is *Dreaming.*
- Farming is *Reproduction.*
- Farming is *Nurturing.*

Cultivating the heart of young people can only occur when leaders have a willingness to endure the process along with a mindset to seek wisdom. After all, there is no other way. Many Youth Leaders are not as effective and result oriented as they could be, because they lack the necessary skills to sow and reap the harvest they long for. They will pray, but even after prayer, there is still the need to do what is essential for proper growth. No wonder the Apostle Paul emphasized this when he said "Be not deceived, God is not mocked. What so ever a man sows, that he shall reap."

The gift you spend most of your time developing is the gift that you will see the most fruits coming from. Stay with me as we explore four critical success factors for growing your youth ministry into the harvest you desire. I call them the youth ministry *"F.A.R.M Principle."*

Finding Them

In his eagerness to share with his brother what he had just experienced, the first thing Andrew did was to find his brother Simon and tell him, "We have found the Messiah." Jesus found Philip the next day and said to him "Follow me." Phillip likewise did the very same thing; he found Nathaniel and told him about Jesus. All that took place in John 1:40-45. What an amazing yet simple way to find youths and spread the message of hope. I call it the *ASPN* plan; Andrew-Simon-Phillip-Nathaniel.

What is the number one thing that every Church, Pastor or Youth Leader seeks? You can think about it for a while, but in the meantime, I will tell you what I came up with. My answer to that question is *"More people."* Without a shadow of a doubt, I am sure that there is a time in every Youth Leader's life when he or she wants to expand the youth ministry numerically.

It is said that quantity speaks volumes. More people in the Church means more everything. At the core of my answer is, of course, evangelism. More than anything else, God wants us to seek and find those who are not within the fold. We don't have to look hard to see dying youths around us. They are everywhere.

Chapter 15 of Luke is decorated with stories relating to the lost and found. The shepherd had to find his sheep; the woman had to find her coin and father found his son who came back home. Jesus shared these stories to advocate mercy, mainly because the Pharisees in the crowd were disgruntled at his passion for the lost. Note that at the end of each story, there was merriment. The words "Rejoice" and "Celebrate" keep recurring to reflect the intentionality of action and a sense of completion.

Youth Leaders are likewise summoned to find lost youths in our communities and by extension, our nation and the world. It is our mandate to find more people to come and be a part of the kingdom. Youths are no different. We should seek to find them at any cost. Regardless of the state of our youths, there are ways to locate them. Sometimes they may not be what we expect them to be, but that is for God to decide, not us.

David in 1 Samuel chapter 22 was astonished at what he found when God sent 400 men for him to be their commander and for them to eventually help him in battle as he continued running from King Saul. The Bible says "David left Gath and escaped to the cave of Adullam. When his brothers and his father's household heard about it, they went down to him there. All those who were in distress or debt or discontented gathered around him, and he became their commander. About four hundred men were with him." David must have been concerned about the men who started following him. It had to take some amount of grace to lead the indebted, distressed and disconnected, but not long after, they were known as *David's Mighty Men*.

I remember when I was Youth Leader for my local church, I got tired of seeing the same faces coming night after night. It's not that I never wanted to see those who were always coming, I just felt in my heart that we needed to get out of the building and go find the youths out in the community. I loved my youth group, and they knew that fact, but I was uncomfortable with the little or no progress that we were making in regards to finding new people. I expressed my concerns to my committee and further to the group at large, and they understood my position, so we set out on a path to find new faces. I knew we had interested youths out there in the community and wanted to discover them.

We started a community youth club, Saturday morning sports ministry with the young men and many nights of what we called Food, Fun and Fellowship *"triple F"*. We had talent competitions for weeks and registered with the Jamaica 4H Club which allowed us to partake in social development activities and events such as cooking competitions with other community clubs. These are just some of the things we did to undertake the mission of finding youths in our surroundings at the time.

It was never an easy task. We had to develop a strategic way of doing so and stuck to them most of the time. Finding the youths in your surrounding can be a challenge, especially if they are approached in the wrong way. While each area has unique dynamics and obstacles, the model of love remains as Jesus did it. Jesus was a servant leader who acted in the spirit of love as he sought after men, women, youth and children. With this in mind, we formulated a practical way that worked for me as a Youth Leader, and I hope it will help you and your youth ministry too. We found youths by expressing an attitude of L.O.V.E.

Lowliness – To act in a manner of humility and meekness as you seek them.

Organize- To integrate them into the youth group.

Validate– To let them know that they have made the right choice in being apart.

Encourage– To see in them what they can't see as yet.

Many are afraid to take on the responsibility or the task to find this young generation. The deliberate act to find and invite youth to come and be a part of a life-changing phenomenon began to pay off. It was a joined effort with the entire youth ministry and me. We started to move from a few youths on a given night to almost 100 youths during our youth ministry nights. Now that we had such numbers, what was our next move going to be? That will take us into the next phase of the F.A.R.M principle: accommodating them.

Accommodate Them

Your role as a Youth Leader is to bring order and stability to your youth ministry. Your duty in this phase of the *F.A.R.M* principle has to be more of a facilitator. There will be massive trafficking sometimes based on the frequent influx of those found and added to the group. Now the question is, how do you balance the group? I had to ask myself that question, and I sought answers.

My youth ministry was not only growing, but it became more of a mixed group with both Churched and Un-Churched youths, and some of the youths we found had severe behavioural challenges. That was something we needed to start working on quickly. Some of our older youths didn't like the new challenge at all. We had to find a way to merge the two groups into one body of youths. We also had to remind the youths who were already there that this was what we call "friendship evangelism."

This part can be very frustrating for many Youth Leaders. Although the vision was communicated with my Pastor and other leaders of the Church, there have been a few time when I had to stand up in meetings and defend said vision because of a few persons who were in disagreement with the vision. As was stated before, other occupants may not always understand the strategies of the youth ministry and the extent to which Youth Leaders have to accommodate disrespectful and misbehaving youths. Do not be too hasty to dismiss the critics. Sometimes it will help you to reconstruct the plan and move forward.

The Youth Leader now stands between a rock and a hard place as he or she accommodates them, but this can be solved, so there is no need to panic. You already succeeded in getting the newcomers to visit your youth ministry and placed them in the frame of mind to be impacted by you and your group so then it's time to engage them into things that will bring the transformation.

This is the nurturing personality of the farmer. You have already sown the seed, and now you have to engage yourself in watering and facilitating the right amount of exposure to sunlight. Using the analogy here will give a better understanding of this stage. Keep in mind that while the newly found youth is showing up, he or she is not fully mature as yet. Just as excess water and sunlight can damage a young tree, so it is that too much exposure, expectation and pressure can cause these youths to withdraw themselves from the newly found environment of the youth ministry.

Be patient with them and trust God that He will minister to them as you do your part. "I planted the seed, Apollos watered, but only God has been making it grow", says the Apostle Paul to the Corinthian Church. Paul used the analogy of physical farming, alluding to them, a spiritual investment concerning the growth and development of God's Church. That is the only way it works, only if each person is faithful to his or her role.

Accommodating newly found youths and their behavioural challenges will always be an essential skill of a Youth Leader and the youth ministry. Here are ten (10) ways to accommodate them without letting them feel uncomfortable while in the process.

- Be *Non-judgmental* toward their reactions.
- Be *Trustworthy* toward their confessions.
- Be *Understanding* toward their interpretations.
- Be *Supportive* of their aspirations.
- Be *Mindful* toward their background.
- Be *Firm* yet graceful.
- Be *Gentle*.
- Be *Quick* to listen.
- Be *Observant* in all areas.
- Be *kind* but wise.

I have been asked many times about the number of young people who are a part of the Ministry I lead. Operation Youth Reap is an evangelism and discipleship medium to bring youths into the kingdom. When we began, it was not an easy task. Some of the things I did in the church building to attract youths were often criticized. Few complained about the building being messed up, but I continued nevertheless, under the careful supervision, of course. Fight for your youths. Make them feel like your youth ministry is where they belong because they do belong there. This reminds me of two young men from the community of Wood Hall, Clarendon, Jamaica. They stood on the outside of the church, and when the service came to an end, they said they wanted to join the REAP team because "we make Christianity look like fun." They were not yet believers in the faith but what struck me was the fact that they realized that they had a place in the kingdom of God. A place they just might fit into.

Reach Them

"Save one", Batman said to Flash, in DC's Justice League movie. "Then what?" Flash replied. He had never been in that level of combat before. "You will know what to do. Just save one," Batman continued. In the end, Flash rescued all nine people who were being held hostage by the evil villain Stephano.

The very first time I saw this scene in the movie, I immediately thought about our reaction to God's command to reach those who need saving. Flash never had the slightest idea or the ability to fight. In his words, he only pushed a few people and ran away. He was underestimating his potential. His involvement in the rest of the movie stood paramount to the sues of the justice league team, including electrocuting the mother box to resurrect the deceased Clarke Kent, *Superman,* from the dead, saving Wonder Woman from a devastating hit, saving a Russian family from being killed and many more actions that contributed to saving the world.

While seeing the crisis, he found his strength to reach and save those around him. Youth Leaders do not possess abilities such as fictional superheroes do, but we contribute to the greater good of humanity when we make an effort to reach youths who are held captive by the entrapment of their era.

Many youth-based organizations around the world started out of a crisis. One such movement is Youth for Christ. Youth for Christ (YFC) has a distinctive history of youth evangelism. In the early 1940s during World War II, many young men, mostly ministers and evangelists, held large rallies in Canada, England and the United States. As the hunger for God's Word grew, it became evident that there needed to be someone to coordinate this movement, providing leadership, developing strategies and coordinating speakers, musicians and locations.

Beginning in dozens of cities at the end of World War II, YFC quickly organized into a national movement. Billy

Graham became YFC's first full-time staff member. From the mid-1940s through the mid-1950s, YFC grew rapidly and spun off several other organizations, including the Billy Graham Evangelistic Association, World Vision International, Greater Europe Mission, Overseas Crusades, and Gospel Films.

It was during this time that the famous YFC rallies took place, where thousands of youth, young adults, and middle-aged people turned out on Saturday nights to hear famous preachers, movie stars, musicians, and others. From the mid-1950s through the mid-1960s, YFC turned its focus to teenagers.

In Canada, the organization initiated Bible clubs, created Lifeline (a ministry to teen delinquents), ran teen talent contests, started Bible quiz games, sent Teen Teams overseas, and used camping trips to spread the gospel. After the mid-1960s, YFC discovered a few things. Teenagers were changing, and programs had to be changed to meet their needs. YFC began sharing more material between chapters and developed better training strategies for its staff. Youth for Christ also refocused its energy on unchurched teenagers – reaching and 'discipling' them with personal attention.

The late 70s saw the high-energy leadership of Brian Stiller as President. This vibrant leader featured an emphasis on the recruitment and training of young men and women in developing excellence in leadership. This period also saw a new commitment to the church through a special effort to enlist the general public through TV Specials.

The '80s and '90s were characterized by a strong sense of vision and a "whatever it takes" philosophy, seeking Canada's unreached youth. Junior Varsity, a ministry that reached out to junior high youth and Street-Level Outreach ministering to kids who are troubled at home, school or on the streets was initiated. The main focus of this Street-level outreach was drop-in centres that continue to emerge across Canada. There was a renewed emphasis on large group events such as Christian concerts that had a strong evangelistic thrust. Music and drama teams made a comeback with approximately seven chapters using this form of ministry regularly. Project Serve, a combined evangelism/work project ministry to third world countries, took off dramatically with teams of teens and adults serving abroad. Ministries stemming from the chapters included drop-in centres, campus Life programs, teen moms outreach and support, institutional ministries, urban street youth ministry, missions trips/work projects, bus ministries, sports outreach events, crisis line support, music groups and discipleship growth groups. Youth for Christ and its efforts to reach youths across the world has been making highly useful today.

There is still a great call for Youth Leaders with a vision to serve and reach our lost youths. Sometimes we might not recognize the urge to do so; however, here are five reasons to consider when wondering what to do about helping in the harvest and reaching youths in your community.

- You see the **Crisis-** The disciples appointed deacons. (Act 6:1-3)
- You heard the **Call-** God called the boy Samuel. (1Samuel 3:4-10)
- You carry the **Burden-** Nehemiah wept for days. (Nehemiah 1:4)
- You are **Competent** -Paul worked with Aquila & Priscilla because he was a tentmaker as they were. (Acts 18:2-3)
- You are **Passionate-** Lydia persuaded Paul and Silas to stay at her home so she could show kindness to them. (Acts 16:14-15)

Some may ask, what is the difference between finding and reaching? There are differences. You can find something without reaching for it. Reaching youths, in this case, means deliberately extending an arm to pull closer to one's self and for empowerment.

Getting to know young people should be a worthwhile adventure; it should involve not just meeting their spiritual needs, but also impacting every aspect of their lives. Whenever I call youths to check on their wellbeing, my first question is not about church or why I didn't see him or her on Sunday or youth ministry night. Instead, I ask them questions about themselves and those around them.

I ask about school, family, hobbies etc. As their Youth Leader, you should attend their graduations, family funerals and other events that they may invite you to be a part of. Celebrate their achievements with them. Like adults, your youths are also made up of body, soul and spirit. Do not take an interest only in their spiritual lives. This might give them the impression that you are only interested in church-related issues. This can also cause them to think that the Youth Leader is shallow and impossible to connect with, and soon they will become even more distant.

Mentor Them

I quietly sat there, waiting for the session to be over. It was a two-week mentorship seminar sponsored by the National Integrity Action, and I was exhausted after three hours of PowerPoint and discussions. Four of my mentees joined me at the seminar. It was a grand opportunity, so they made use of it.

The moderator ended by asking a few questions and promised to give incentives in the form of phone cards. She wanted two young men to step forward. They quickly jumped up, and she managed to identify two of my mentees. "What is mentoring?" she asked. Smith skillfully explained and got his phone card and headed back to his seat. Next question, "Who can say they have a mentor in their life and explain how it has impacted you?" She identified Nigel, my other mentee. "Well, I have a mentor and meeting him changed my life. I was on my way to kill someone the day I met him. He spoke into my life, and ever since that moment, he has been there for me. Some weeks ago, while he was in South Africa, he sent me a message that I got at minutes after 2 am because it's a different time zone. The message read *"How are you my son in whom I am well pleased?"* It did something for me that day because I was feeling discouraged", he expressed. He then turned in my direction, pointed and shouted, "My mentor is sitting right there, there he is, his name is Leroy Hutchinson!"

By now you can imagine the look of surprise on my face. I was shocked beyond words. I knew I had messaged him, but to be honest, I didn't even remember that specific message, but he did. Nigel's reflection on mentorship inspired everyone in the room that day, but most of all, I believe it punched out any doubts I had about my decision to mentor young people. The moderator then said, "Leroy, stand up and come for a phone card too."

Why Mentoring- Mentoring is the fourth and final phase of the youth ministry F.A.R.M principle. The Youth Leader would have already found new people, discovered ways to make them feel at home and reached out to their needs. It is now time to deposit and invest in them. Mentoring is needed because of the social, emotional, psychological, academic and spiritual needs of our youths today. Mentoring has been an internationally recognized way of helping young people.

Global Mentor and Psychologist Courtney Richards says, "The type of mentoring that is being proposed is what we term "whole life mentoring" where one person invests his or life and resources in another to help transform their lives for the better." Reverend Richards believes that this mentoring takes a holistic approach and provides a "big sister/big brother" or parent model to help children and youth grow and develop into mature citizens who contribute to the building up of their lives, communities, schools, and society. "We are convinced that our youth require the following three critical inputs in their lives to rescue them from the dysfunctionalities of their era." He concluded by saying, "Our youths today need the following three things:

- They need significant **healing relationships**.
- They need a sense of **mission or purpose** - something larger than themselves - to invest their lives in. This will help give them focus on their lives and to help them realize their God-given potential.
- They need **moral and ethical** grounding built on the word of God with a system of accountability to help ensure that they stay true to God's ideals for them."

The Youth Leader who mentors his or her youth group will always be one step ahead of those who don't. Being a leader is not the same as being a mentor. Mentoring is a decision, a choice to invest in another intentionally. Mentoring is deliberate. Mentoring is an investment, and mentoring is rewarding. I believe there are three similarities in starting a new bank account. These are three (3) things that every Youth Leader must know about the process of becoming a mentor.

Be Deliberate - Your deliberate approach to mentoring will have to be fierce and compassionate at the same time. In my years as a Youth Leader, I have had the privilege of being approached and mentored by several individuals. It was a deliberate approach taken by Pastor Victolyn Howden at McCook's Pen, Bishop Junior Headlam at a Parish Youth Retreat, and as I shared in my other book *"Purpose Has No Shame"*, Rev. Courtney Richard's approach at the seminar. They all knew what they were getting into, but they also knew that if they were going to help me through the journey of my life in a more effective way, then it had to be an intentional approach.

'Behind every successful sprinter, there is a brilliant coach.' That was a tribute to Coach Glen Mills, coach for world record holder and fastest man on the planet, Usain Bolt. If we truly see the importance of mentoring, coaching and shaping the next generation, we will have far more great moments in our communities, churches and schools. The mentor empowers a person to see a possible future, and believe it can be obtained. That was precisely what Jesus did with Peter in Luke chapter 5 as he calls His first disciple to join Him in starting the Church. Further on in the Gospels, we see Jesus approaching many more young men with the same attitude.

The Jesus Model -David Paul Kirkpatrick, in an article entitled *Jesus' Bachelors* wrote, "Jesus' twelve disciples were probably young, almost all under the age of eighteen and some as young as 15. All were most likely bachelors, but for one. There is no indicator in Scripture of a specific age for any disciple; so we look through the lens of historical context as well as clues derived from Scripture.

In the time of Jesus, a Jewish man received a wife after the age of 18. Peter was the only one known to have been married. In Matthew 8:14-15, we learn that Peter had a wife when Jesus healed his mother-in-law. Again, scripturally, no other disciples' wives are mentioned.

Why are we to assume that Jesus' disciples were so young? The tradition of education at that time indicates it. Education for the Jewish child concluded at the age of 15. For those bright (or wealthy) enough, higher education consisted of studying under a local rabbi. If they didn't find a rabbi that accepted them as a student (much like a college entrance application), then they entered the workforce by their mid-teens. In most cases, they apprenticed under their fathers and worked for the prosperity of the family.

Most of the disciples were already apprenticing at their trades as in the case of disciples, James and John. Historically, a rabbi of that time would begin to take on students at the age of 30. It was at the age of 30 that Jesus, we believe, began his public ministry. This also fits in with the rabbinical traditions of the time.

Why was Jesus considered outlandish by the status quo? He was not a rabbi who taught in the synagogue. He taught by the seashore and from the mountaintop. He was anti-religious. His message was radical. Jesus' idea of loving everyone occurred to no one. The culture was about hate and aggression. Also, Jesus stated that He was the Son of God. He claimed that the only way to God was through him. (John 14:6)

Of course, this posse of young Jewish guys was not known as "Christians". Most probably, they were simply students of the Rabbi, Jesus of Nazareth. As far as we can ascertain from the book of Acts, the early Jesus movement was known as "The Way" (Acts 9:2; Acts 24:14). The name "Christianity" did not occur until several years after Jesus' resurrection in a place called Antioch. (Acts 11:27)

Unlike the filmic portrayals of the past and even those in the latest TV miniseries of the Bible airing now, the disciples were probably not middle-aged men. Not only is it against the ancient times but flies in the face of Scripture. The only one who might have been older, other than Peter, was Matthew. He had a profession as a tax collector.

Here are a few youth indicators from Scripture:

The use of the term "little ones."

In Matthew 11:25, Luke 10:21, and John 13:33, Jesus calls his disciples little children, "little ones". This would be a bit insulting if they were men, no matter how radical or gentle the rabbi!

James and John

These guys were brothers. They had a pushy mom named Salome who wanted to arrange where they would sit with Jesus at the table. Salome's pushiness wouldn't make sense if the brothers were grown, men. (Matthew 20:20-24). Jesus nicknamed them "Sons of

Thunder" as they were probably either loud or bold, characteristics typically found in youth.

Jesus must have been the most excellent mentor I know. His strategic plan to empower youths in his time was fascinating.

The Investment- The fact that mentoring is an investment it means that should the mentoring relationship fail, it will bring you pain just like any other meaningful relationship. Make a note of the word investment because that is exactly what mentoring is all about, and if the fruits of your investment fail, it will feel like you have lost big time.

That was how I felt with my first mentee Denver Gayle. Having the franchise of working with him offered me a sense hope that he would grow into a man and that time spent would bring significant change in his life. I was in my early 20s and had started investing in him when he was 15 years old. I approached him and told him I wanted to be his mentor. My intention was a long term, not for a short period. We found him, accommodated him as he joined our youth ministry, reached him and then began the mentoring process after a few months. He was a young man of promise and potential. He was an extraordinary footballer with a teachable attitude, so after two years of mentorship, I appointed him Sports Director for the organization; Operation Youth Reap. I invested time, energy, counsel and much more in the young man.

We had plans for the ministry, and I believe God had great plans for his life too, but on an evening in November 2012, Denver was in a car accident on the Old Harbour main road and that was the end. He died tragically. I wept bitterly and asked God a tonne of questions. The pain of losing a mentee is unexplainable. I know this to be true because I have lost mentees through death and other avenues.

Investing in youths can be a risky business, but it will be worth it. The sudden loss of my mentee Denver taught me a few valuable lessons on mentoring as I reflected on our relationship. Here are ten (10) things you need to know about being a mentor when deciding to invest in the lives of others.

- Mentors **Guide**
- Mentors **Teach**
- Mentors **Reassure**
- Mentors **Model**
- Mentors **Protect**
- Mentors **Observe**

* Mentors **Envision**
* Mentors **Connect**
* Mentors **Support**
* Mentors **Rebuke**

Reap The Rewards–Before I started mentoring Leyon Lindo, he was an angry young man who, in his own words "wanted to inflict pain and hurt to others." He had no vision for his life; neither could he identify his true potential. The night I met Leyon, he accepted Jesus through one of our Operation Youth Reap weekend missions and ever since we started a mentoring relationship. I have been mentoring him and taking him on various mission trips across Jamaica. Lyon has found a new passion so much so that he has been giving himself to the service others in sports outreach, street witnessing and being a mentor himself. Today Leyon is enrolled at the G.C. Foster College in Jamaica, doing a Bachelor's Degree in Physical Education and Sports.

A successful Youth Leader has to see his or her youths as prospects for greatness at all times. See people for who they can become and not just who they are at the moment. Leyon Lindo is one of many young men that I am mentoring and training to become a mentor themselves. My ultimate aim is to help these young men and women excel in whatever they were created to do, but whether or not my mentees excel in their different fields, I take great pleasure in being a mentor to them.

Here are 11 Biblical models of mentoring relationships where we see an older person investing in a younger and the benefits they reaped afterwards.

Mentoring Relations	Results
Jethro & Moses	**Moses** delivered Israel from slavery
Moses &Joshua	**Joshua** led Israel after Moses died
Jesus &His disciples	**The Disciples** took the Gospel around the world & caused the church to expand and continue to grow up to today
Elijah & Elisha	**Elisha** became the next Prophet
Eli & Samuel	**Samuel** became the next Prophet
Paul &Timothy	**Timothy** became a young Pastor

Paul &Titus	**Titus** was a Young Leader
Naomi &Ruth	**Ruth** was the Grandmother of King David.
Mordecai &Esther	**Esther** became Queen of Persia who risked her life for the survival of the Jewish nation
Priscilla /Aquila & Apollos	**Apollos** was taught the gospel eloquently
Deborah & Bakar	**Bakar's** troop defeated Sisera

Make An Effort- Over the years working with various youth ministries and within Operation Youth Reap, we have seen many fruits of the mentoring initiative. The Operation Youth Reap seeks to recruit and mobilize suitable persons from across the spectrum of the society to walk alongside selected youths from different schools, communities and churches. This is to help them to confront the issues that are preventing them from being productive, successful and well-adjusted students as well as well-developed persons.

Our youth today are faced with problems in the home, schools and the society at large. Some of the issues and factors include stress, developmental issues, popular culture, religious issues and current affairs.

Mentoring is about inviting people into our lives so we can pour into them. Mentoring can be an inconvenient relationship. Inviting people in your life can be dangerous, mainly because you may attract people with different motives.

It is critical that as a Youth Leader, you ask yourself this one question "Is my life worth following?" Mentoring is about demonstrating a progressive pattern and encouraging youths to do as you are doing. In the words of Paul the Apostle "Follow my example as I follow the example of Christ" (1 Corinthians 11:1 NIV).

Your Winning Attitudes

"If your desire is to win, then total reliance on God is always your best chance in your approach to Youth Leadership. It is the star player in your game; it is your M.V.P. and must be seen as such at all times. Being a Youth Leader is a major deal, so everything you do has to be from a perspective of complete surrender to God and Him alone. That is how we will win."- Leroy Hutchinson

S ome described it as a miracle, others were too stunned to speak, but it is known by many as one of the greatest comebacks in football's history. Like many Barcelona fans around the world, I was watching this match out of loyalty to my team. I sat there, glued to my laptop while keeping a friend updated on the scores at the same time. My heart was racing; beating to the rhythm of what felt like a bass drum inside my chest. I tried to convince myself that it was possible. "We can still win" I kept on repeating, but I wasn't sure I had bought into it.

Barcelona needed five clear goals to win. On paper, it was an impossible task. The reporters said, "It will be a very hard mission for FC Barcelona as they will try to overturn their first leg 4-0 loss in Paris against PSG. In the history of the Champions League, no club who has lost by a 4-0 score in their first leg matchup has been able to progress in the competition, so this is why PSG have to be confident."

The match was on its way, and Barcelona had led 2-0 at the break after just three minutes. As the match progressed, the Spanish champions were 5-3 down on aggregate in the 88th minute but scored three goals in the final seven minutes in one of the greatest European ties of all time. Neymar's free-kick and penalty followed by

Sergi Roberto's 95th-minute winner sealed victory on an incredible night at the Nou Camp.

The match was incredibly intense, and no one could believe the outcome at the end of the game. Barcelona 6 goals and PSG- 5. Barcelona made Champions League history by becoming the first team to overturn a first-leg 4-0 deficit as they knocked out Paris St-Germain to reach the quarter-finals for the 10th successive season. By far, that was the best football match I have ever watched in my lifetime.

Most Valuable Players

Our battle for this generation is similar to that of a great comeback in a thrilling and breathtaking football game. To the natural eyes and the spectators, it looks like an impossible task. To the analysts, it is an uphill climb. To the faint-hearted, it is a hopeless case, but I implore you to hold on, do not give up hope, because the end has not yet come. We have gone through nine chapters together so far, but there is still a bright light at the end of this tunnel. We can still win them.

The culture and its challenges are pushing forcefully at those who are brave enough to fight back and trying to impact the youths in today's society. The oppositions are mounting and time seems like it's winding up. People are beginning to walk out of the stands, and heads are being held down. Never in the history of the world have we ever seen such a wayward generation. Yet I echo these words to you, my reader, we can still win. Notice I said we because this needs teamwork. After careful thinking, I have garnered the three most valuable players in the form of victorious attitudes that every Youth Leader would need in order to win back this generation. I call them your *"Dream Team."*

Dream Team

Player #1– Reliance On God

If you desire to win, total reliance on God is always the best chance in your approach to Youth Leadership. It is the star player in your game; it is your M.V.P. and must be seen as such at all times. Being a Youth Leader is a major deal, so everything you do has to be from a perspective of complete surrender to God and Him alone. That is how we will win.

 I have been approached by Youth Leaders on more than one occasion, asking me many questions about youth ministry but the question on how to handle frustration appears most frequent of them all. Many ask: "How do you serve as Youth Leader without being frustrated?" Well, I don't have a blueprint on how to deal with frustration, but I consider the many factors which may ultimately lead to frustration. Here are a few suggestions that will prevent you from going down the pathway of frustration and allow you to keep depending on God to help you in your journey as a Youth Leader.

A Pure Heart – A pure heart is not necessarily a perfect heart. God is not looking for perfect leaders. "The most important quality of a leader in ministry is a pure heart. A heart the leader allows God to change, mould and reshape according to His will," says Doug Field. There is always an advantage to any leader who allows God to work on their heart. He is looking for leaders whose thoughts and deeds He can remodel.

Time Management - A.W. Tozer remarked, "If a man wants to be used by God, he cannot spend all his time with people." The time we spend with God is an imperative factor that leads to complete dependence on His will. Leaders have to set aside quality time, not just for prayer but also for meditation and solitude. The Youth Leader whose schedule God not only fits into but controls is always at an advantage in ministry. He or she will rely on God's timing in every area of life.

Adaptability- While I was a local Youth Leader at my Church, we had a decision to make. My committee and I realized that the attendance of the youths was way below the usual so we did an evaluation. At the end of the assessment, we found out that the youths had an issue with the Wednesday evening meeting time. We had been meeting on Wednesday nights for the past six years, and we had gotten accustomed to that particular weekday. My team and I recognized that things had changed and so we had to compromise and strike a balance too. We changed it to Friday nights, and everyone was now finding it way more convenient than before.

Being adaptable to circumstances is another critical facet you will need as you depend on God entirely to grow in Youth Leadership. Changes, disappointments, failures, critics, and discouragements will create all breed frustration, but only if you allow them to do so. If you can't adapt to these setbacks, then you most likely won't succeed as a Youth Leader. Adaptability in this context means that you are always prepared to do it God's way and not your way.

A Teachable Spirit - In order to learn, one must be willing to embrace knowledge, but to be teachable one must be willing to unlearn and relearn. Erwin G. Hall puts it this way, "An open mind is the beginning of self-discovery and growth. We can't learn anything new until we can admit that we don't already know everything. In other words, teachable leaders will be able to give others the chance to influence their development positively. "I have not already obtained all things," said the Apostle Paul to the Philippian Church. Paul was a great Christian leader with the ability to learn, unlearn and relearn. He was a profound example of what a teachable leader looks like.

Everyone we meet has something to teach us; we just need to pay attention. Leaders won't always have the answers, therefore becoming more teachable to God and anyone else from whom you can gain wisdom is a sign of total reliance, but not on one's self. John Maxwell explained, "If you want to grow and learn, you must approach as many things as you can as a beginner, not an expert." As a Youth Leader, you will find yourself learning from your young people sometimes. Don't be afraid of that; they can teach you a whole lot.

Player #2 - Teamwork

Some years ago, I was leading an Operation Youth Reap Mission with a team of young people in Ocho Rios, Jamaica, for the weekend. We got up early Saturday morning to engage the young men in the community with sports ministry. The team and I had an excellent time, after which we decided to refresh ourselves in a nearby river in the area. By now, everyone who knows me knows that I'm not a swimmer. Notice, I didn't say "good swimmer", that's because I cannot swim. All the guys were having fun in the water except me. I was there recording everything on my phone. I suddenly felt an eagerness to go in and especially because the team wanted me to join in the fun. The problem was, my inability to swim never came up in that group. Nobody had that information.

It somehow slipped my mind to enquire about the depth of the water and also to update the team on my inability to swim. From the look of things, I thought they were all standing on the surface of the pool, so I dived in with no one else in the water at the time and then the rest of the story was history. The water was eight feet high, which was, of course above my head by over two feet! I was shocked, appalled and panicking all at the same time.

Adding to all that, I began calling for help, and the guys thought I was faking it. That made it even worse. I thought I would drown, but I never gave up, I kept on praying and trying. I kept on signalling for help with my hand so as not to take in any more water until one of the teammates finally recognized that I wasn't playing. He jumped in. They all jumped in to save me. In his effort to grab me, one person dislocated his shoulder and had to be rescued by another as well. In the end, we were all holding on to a tree stump that stretched across the river, looking at each other and breathing sighs of relief.

I saw myself in a body bag that morning before they jumped in. Three minutes of what felt like a disaster in one way; but a life lesson for me in another. When it was all over, we sat down together, gave thanks to God and reflected on the lessons learned that morning, before heading back to the church for breakfast.

As we sat and reflected, one team member who was primarily instrumental in saving my life told us that he was hesitant about coming to the weekend mission, but he heard the voice of God saying "the team needs you this weekend." I will forever be grateful to these guys: Delano Thompson, Hojay Nugent, Jowayne Francis and Seymour Mcnab. That day, they selflessly demonstrated what teamwork was all about.

In our discussion that morning, we observed a few lessons learned about teamwork. Here are ten (10) benefits of building an effective team to help you as a Youth Leader.

- Teamwork reminds you that you have *Help*.

- Teamwork is *Effective*.
- Teamwork will **Save** you.
- Teamwork is an indication of a **Secure Leader**.
- Teamwork shares the **Load**.
- Teamwork creates **Unity**.
- Teamwork preserves **Strength**.
- Teamwork invites others to be a part of the **Vision**.
- Teamwork creates an opportunity for **Growth**.
- Teamwork measures the effectiveness of a **Leader**.

Leaders are never independent of teamwork. Being the responsible leader I deemed myself to be; I was still a bit annoyed for the rest of the day. I was plagued with guilt; feeling irresponsible and reckless and pondering how I could have caused the death of myself and a few guys on my team. Overwhelmed and unable to sleep, the Lord said to me "Leroy, today was a true reflection of the imperfections and limitations of men." He reminded me that as leaders, no matter how careful and cautious we try to be, something can and will go against our plan. When this happens, however, that's when you realize the value of help and teamwork. I thought I was their strong leader, but for whatever reason, on that morning, my weakest area was put to the test, thanks be to God, teamwork saved the day.

Player #3 - Provide Hope

This generation is still searching for a reason to fight on. Because of such a reality, Youth Leaders are best described as *merchants of hope*. We hope against hope; we cling to a mere possibility that things will get better and brandish this with an act of faith. The wise man Solomon in Proverbs 13:12 wrote, "Hope deferred makes the heart sick, but a dream fulfilled is a tree of life." In other words, when hope has been diminished, it poses a threat to our success, and it makes reaching our goals even more difficult. Optimism is the reservoir we resort to for rescue when it seems like the conditions are unbearable. Edward S. Ame remarked, "Hope is an outreaching desire with an expectancy of good. It is a characteristic of all living beings." Your youth ministry needs all the optimism it can get from your leadership. No one wants to follow a leader with a negative attitude. Youths want to know that the person leading them will never throw in the towel. Hope is always one step ahead of failure. It is said that the "Heights of great men reached and kept were not attained by sudden flight but they, while their companions slept, were upward toiling through the night."

In the same way, hopeful Youth Leaders never surrender. Hopeful Youth Leaders stay up while others fall asleep. They are always working towards rebuilding assurance in their youth ministry. Here are ten (10) reasons why every Youth Leader should always try to be a beacon of hope for their youth ministry.

- Hope *Reassures* in doubt.
- Hope *Awakens* in slumber.
- Hope *Revives* in stagnancy.
- Hope *Builds* in brokenness.
- Hope *Loves* despite the hate.
- Hope *Follows* in rebellion.
- Hope *Trusts* in uncertainty.
- Hope *Heals* in wounds.
- Hope *Continues* in halt.
- Hope *Perseveres* in discouragement.

Developing and executing your vision, roles and responsibilities in your youth ministry will have to be connected to these three key game-changers, even if you have learned other strategies. Reliance on God, Inspiring teamwork and providing hope are valuable for you as a Youth Leader.

Winning Is Your Choice

I remember witnessing one of the most inspirational moments I've ever seen, during the Athens' Olympic Games in the summer of 2004. The athlete wept bitterly. They were tears of joy. That day, El Guerrouj's story changed from disappointment to victory all because hope was still within his reach.

In 1996, he had been the favourite in the 1500m final of the Atlanta Olympics. But there he stumbled over the leg of his toughest rival, Noureddine Morceli. The Algerian became the Olympic Champion, El Guerrouj finished twelfth. Four years later someone else came in his way: The Kenyan Noah Ngeny out sprinted El Guerrouj on the home stretch. Between those two Olympic Games, the Moroccan had dominated his distance but still failed to win an Olympic title.

In the summer of 2004, Hicham El Guerrouj travelled to Athens as one of the tragic figures of the Olympic history. He was collecting world records and gold medals at World Championships. Between 1997 and 2003 the Moroccan was the 1500m World Champion four times in a row. Additionally, he won this distance twice at the World Indoor Championships but, in contrast, his Olympic story was a heartbreaking one. Out of forty-six

1500m races he had lost only two, the two Olympic finals. The disappointment was so big that El Guerrouj almost quit his career. Thirty-five days of vacation were not enough to pull him through this trauma. "It was so hard that sometimes I even missed training." El Guerrouj expressed. Three months later, he fulfilled his dream in Athens by winning his first Olympic gold medal at 1500m in an astonishing fashion, and finally, he had achieved everything. His hopes recovered. "Four years ago these were tears of pain, today's tears are of joy," said Hicham El Guerrouj. "At this historical place wherein 1896 the Games took place for the first time is something extraordinary," said Hicham El Guerrouj.

Hicham El Guerrouj returned home with two gold medals, and that had only been achieved by one athlete in the history of the Olympic Games: Paavo Nurmi. The legendary Finn was the double Olympic Champion back in 1924 at 1500m and 5,000m. Another record of Nurmi will remain untouched.

What many people did not know, including me, is that winning the 1500m final signified the end of an eight-year-old nightmare for Hicham El Guerrouj that day in Athens, Greece. Michael Bautista summed up El Guerrouj's performance this way:

"Hicham El Guerrouj proved today what we all know is possible in humanity. After all those setbacks, all those hardships, and all those disappointments, he comes back today and runs the greatest race of his entire life. The payoff could not be more rewarding for his efforts. Hicham El Guerrouj became the Olympic champion today. By winning the Olympics Men's 1500 meters final, he not only establishes himself as the greatest middle-distance runner in history but also as one of the greatest role models mankind has ever known. Out of all history, how many people have ever shown the type of heart, perseverance, and character that Hicham El Guerrouj has? It's rare to find somebody so dedicated to his sport, so passionate about being the best, and so brave in the face of adversity. After his loss in Atlanta, he came back. After his loss in Sydney, he came back. After his losses this season, he still came back. After being passed in the homestretch today in the race, he came back. After all the deep wounds, the crushing losses, and the cold tears, he has somehow found the strength within himself to do something extraordinary. In accomplishing his lifelong dream of Olympic Gold, he has shown us what we all must believe anything is possible within our own lives. If Hicham El Guerrouj can do it, then surely we can as well. He is an inspiration to many athletes in showing that if you work hard and never give up, you can achieve monumental feats. Hicham El Guerrouj showed us the heartbreaking lows of defeat, the euphoric highs of victory, but most importantly, the true bravery of humanity. Hicham El Guerrouj is a true champion and The King Of The Mile!"

Like the great athlete El Guerrouj, youth ministry must be a priority and a victory to gain. Youth Leaders must fight to the end. The battle is not an easy task, but your youths are worth it. Keep your head up, pray to God and head toward the finish line like the Apostle Paul did when he said: "I press on toward the goal for the prize of the upward call of God in Christ Jesus." (Philippians 3:14)

Going Beyond Self To Win

In our quest to win young men for the kingdom, my sports ministry team has lost more football matches than we have won. Even though we wanted to win each game, I am careful to remind the team that "it's not about winning the game; it's about winning these young people." Despite losing games, they have grasped the concept of "lose to win." The leader who wins even when he or she has seemingly lost will know what it feels like to go beyond themselves. Going beyond yourself to win the youths of this generation is a paramount priority. It will be self-sacrificing and frustrating at times, but the benefits are beyond this world.

Your selflessness has to show up more often than others, even in prayer. It reminds me of the Scottish Preacher John Knox as he prayed "Give me Scotland or I die." More than anything else, John Knox is known for his prayer. "Knox' prayer was not an arrogant demand, but the passionate plea of a man willing to die for the sake of the pure preaching of the gospel and the salvation of his countrymen." Burke Parsons wrote. I believe John Knox is a real example of a leader going beyond himself.

As a leader of a youth mission organization, the call to go beyond what we know, natural talents and IQ, is also an eye-opener, and the rewards can be fulfilling in the end. We have certainly seen progress on numerous occasions in various communities. Sports Ministry is one such avenue that has taught me how to win youths for Christ. It gives the team a chance to apply patience and keep our eyes on what is most important, their souls. Author Denis Waitley says, "The winner's edge is not in a gifted birth, in a high IQ, or talent. The winner's edge is in the attitude, not aptitude." When Youth Leaders understand that winning is not just about them, their age and their abilities, they will experience real victory.

This is the same attitude that motivated Caleb, who was an 85-year-old man but was still determined to win. Caleb beckoned to Joshua when he said, "Now then, just as the Lord promised, he has kept me alive for forty-five years since the time he said this to Moses, while Israel moved about in the wilderness. So here I am today, eighty-five years old! I am still as strong today as the day Moses sent me out; I'm just as vigorous to go out to battle now as I was then. Now give me this hill country that the Lord promised me that day." Joshua 14:10-12).

So then, I implore you to let this be your heart's desire as a youth worker. We should fiercely pray like Caleb, "Give me this [Generation]." We should place a high value on winning this generation of youths because they are worth it. The clock is ticking away, and the opponent is banking on us to fail. With God as your coach, it is impossible to fail. He has made preparations in the past to ensure that you win and He is still doing so on the pages of this book.

Signs Of A Progressive Youth Leader

Am I in the right ministry? Am I winning as a Youth Leader? Am I impacting lives? Am I growing? How do I know whether or not I am doing a good job? Well, these are frequently asked questions that may come across

242

your mind as a youth ministry worker on your journey to becoming a progressive Youth Leader. Notice I didn't say successful Youth Leader in this case? That's because each youth and youth group is unique and possesses their own challenges and dynamics. Each year, I have been invited to speak to thousands of youths from different churches, camps, schools, communities and sometimes other countries too. They are not all the same. There are differences in age, maturity, culture, nature and nurture; therefore, I am forced to adjust my approach and be realistic in my expectations regarding their responses. I believe chapter 7 has clearly illustrated and exhausted that fact.

The Youth Leader who knows how to readjust will most likely progress on different stages even when they are called upon suddenly. With this notion, the journey never stops, and the Youth Leader keeps developing. I believe everyone wants to know whether or not they are effective either way. This will give individuals a chance to make a worthwhile evaluation, fair assessment and develop on weak areas.

While growth is vital to you as a leader, the question of how personal growth is measured is often asked as well. I have looked at my leadership in youth ministry and what I have learned and modelled over the years concerning being a progressive Youth Leader.

Here are twelve (12) *"signs"* you may want to observe as you evaluate your progress and mature in Youth Leadership.

- You have *Accepted* responsibility.
- You have *Readjusted* your ability.
- You have an *Effective* team in motion.
- You have a *Clear* vision and mission.
- You have *Loyalty* toward the task.
- You *Communicate* well.
- You have established *Trust* on both sides.
- You have *Functionality* in your absence.
- You *Respect* those you lead.
- You *Love* those you lead.
- You *Replicate* yourself.
- You *Improve* yourself.

Every progressive Youth Leader has winning attitudes, whether it's through their personality or how they communicate. There are winning methods that the Youth Leader must find to get the job done. He or she also has to be prepared to share those ways. John Maxwell noted, "A leader knows the way, shows the way and goes the way." Those winning ways are there to be discovered, and they will work for you if you realize them soon enough.

The task is already hard. The progress might be slow but keep going. God will send help. His Spirit will energize us. The fruit of the spirit was given to us so that we can deny who our self-seeking ways. We are selfish men by nature. Sometimes the leader will be the first to arrive and the last one to leave. Such is the role of a progressive Youth Leader. It is never about how we start as Youth Leaders, but how we progress and ultimately finish.

My Final Thoughts

The art of leading young people is one of worthwhile investment; however, it is easier said than done. We have gone through 10 chapters, several key points and inspirational stories so far. We have recapped my journey as a young believer and how Youth Ministry impacted me and fostered my dramatic decision to become a Youth Leader myself. All these are to establish a proposition; we all can improve on becoming a person who invests intentionally in young lives.

Dozens of books and articles have been written and published on this topic, but there is still room for one more. This book was specifically designed to express the importance of being a Youth Leader. My prayer for you is that you will find this book as a tool to revive or bring to life, the *"Youth Leader In You."*

Notes

Chapter One

1. The Holy Bible (New International Version)

Chapter Two

1. Newsner, September 11, 2017, The unsung hero of 9/11- Rick Rescorla, https://www.youtube.com/watch?v=J8XfwZAKPk
2. Pettinger, Tejvan. *"Martin Luther King Biography"*, Oxford, UK. www.biographyonline.net, 11th Feb 2008,http://www.biographyonline.net/politicia ns/american/martin-luther-king.html
3. The Global School Health Survey, 2010
4. World Health Organization, World report on child injury prevention,http://www.who.int/violence_injury_pr evention/child/en/
5. Jamaica, https://www.unicef.org/jamaica/, UNICEF Jamaica - Jamaica Home page
6. Wright Brothers Biography, https://www.notablebiographies.com/We-

Z/Wright-Brothers.html, Encyclopedia of World Biography.

7. Lev Grossman, Wednesday, Dec. 15, 2010, PERSON OF THE YEAR 2010, Mark Zuckerberg, http://content.time.com/time/person-of-the-year/2010/

Chapter Three

Strategic Marketing and Technology Solution, WHY IS BRANDING IMPORTANT? Published on March 10, 2017, in Branding, Marketing, Strategy, https://strategynewmedia.com/why-is-branding-important/

Chapter Four

The Gladiator, 2000https://www.rottentomatoes.com/m/gladiator/

Chapter Five

1. Famous Blind and Vision Impaired Persons, https://www.disabled-world.com/artman/publish/famous-blind.shtml, Disabled World

2. Lenstore, Vision Hub,
   https://www.lenstore.co.uk/eyecare/vision-
   without-sight-three-tales-inspiring-blind-p

Chapter Six

1. What is the prayer of Jabez?
   http://www.gotquestions.org/prayer-of-
   Jabez.html, GotQuestions.org
2. Holy Bible, King James Version
3. Our Story & Core Values - Seattle, Wenatchee,
   Redmond, http://www.keymethods.com/about-
   us/story-core-values/, Key Methods
4. http://www.burjkhalifa.ae/en/the-
   tower/factsandfigures.aspx
5. Recent Gems,
   https://www.onlythebible.com/Bible-Gems/wise-
   man-built-on-the-rock.html, The Wise Man, and
   the Foolish Man - Where is Your Foundation?
6. The True Story of Thanksgiving,
   https://www.desiringgod.org/articles/the-true-
   story-of-thanksgiving, Desiring God

Chapter Seven

1. 15- to 17-year-olds: Ages and stages of youth
   development,

http://msue.anr.msu.edu/news/15_to_17_year_ol
ds_ages_and_stages_of_youth_development h,
MSU Extension

2. United Nations Department of Economic and
Social Affairs (UNDESA),
ttp://www.un.org/esa/socdev/documents/youth/f
act-sheets/youth-definition.pdf

3. WHAT DO 21ST-CENTURY CHRISTIAN
YOUTH NEED?,
http://klangchurchofchrist.org/what-do-21st-
century-christian-youth-need, Klang Church Of
Christ

Chapter Nine

1. www.yfc.net

2. Jesus' Bachelors – The Disciples Were Most
Likely Under The Age of 18,
http://www.davidpaulkirkpatrick.com/2013/03/2
5/jesus-bachelors-the-disciples-were-most-likely-
under-the-age-of-18/, David Paul Kirkpatrick's
Living In The Metaverse

Chapter Ten

www.kingofthemie.com

Write a letter to your Youth Leader and say why you think he or she is the best Youth Leader.

_____

_____

_____

_____

_____

_____

_____

_____

_____

_____

_____

_____

_____

_____

_____

_____

_____

_____

Another Book by Leroy Hutchinson

Made in the USA
Columbia, SC
06 July 2021